NLP FOR LIFE SUCCESS

FROM NEGATIVES TO POSITIVES

A SIMPLIFIED EXTRACT FOR HIGH PERFORMERS

MOHAMMED IQBAL B.Tech. (Chemical)

To my beloved ones and great mentors

To whom I shall remain indebted

For providing the foundation

On which this book is based

ISBN 978-1-8381277-9-4 (Paperback)
ISBN 978-1-8381277-8-7 (e-book)

Editing by Proofreadingpal.com.

Table of Contents

Book Summary

Your body and mind may often work in mysterious ways, but they no longer need to be out of your control. Luck is not what determines whether you are successful in life—contrary to popular belief, you get to guarantee it for yourself. If you have ever wondered about the stepping stones to a successful and peaceful happy life, look no further! This book is your one guide to all things positive, while simultaneously helping you rejuvenating your existence though various scientific and psychologically motivating techniques.

Neuro-Linguistic Programming or NLP may sound like an ominous term, but once you acquaint yourself with it, you will see that it is a sure-shot pathway to being motivated, getting in touch with your passions, fixing your goals, and, most importantly, discovering yourself. With NLP, you will be able to programme your brain to communicate with your body and flood it with thoughts and plans to overcome a vast range of hurdles –anxiety, obsessive thoughts, issues in interpersonal relations, goal-setting, work-life balance, negativity, finding the energy to perform daily tasks to dealing with phobias, readjusting your perceptions, addiction and even issues related to professional engagements and business acumen.

NLP helps you find the methods and techniques that work the best for YOU. It provides a comprehensive process to help you identify your needs and desires and then work towards achieving them by creating a safe and affirming space for your mind, body and soul. It provides you with the energy and encouragement to face your deepest fears on your own to become a strong and well-rounded individual, capable of tackling anything life throws at you.

You may often find yourself in tricky and difficult-to-navigate situations at various stages of your existence, but that does not mean you have to be stumped by them. You can rise above the mundane and take any shortcomings in stride. By using the proper NLP techniques for each situation, you can learn to believe in the power of your individuality and soar to the peak of success and contentment, never needing to depend on luck or others. With *NLP for Life Success*, your fate is in your control.

Author Profile

Mohammed Iqbal was born on 19 August 1972, and he completed his education in Chennai, South India, at Shanmugha College of Engineering. Formally a chemical engineer, he has always been keen on sharing his views and knowledge, gathered through his reading and training, to benefit anyone who might be interested in his thoughts.

Like many of us born into middle-class families, he experienced the trauma of family issues, struggle for existence and difficulties in climbing the organisational ladder. However, even though negative impacts pulled at his focus, he successfully managed to overcome all hurdles. He firmly believes, "Without the proper mind training, one can never know how to be a positive and successful person". It is hard to help a person become healthy and socially responsible, but every human has a responsibility to perpetuate progress and personal growth. The realisation that one should share the experience, knowledge and lessons gained during life's journey prompted the author to compile this book.

He is happily married and blessed with two children.

Acknowledgments

Any accomplishment requires the effort of many people, and this work is no different.

I thank my sons and especially my wife, whose patience and support was influential in accomplishing this task.

I thank my friends, whose diligent efforts made this publication possible.

My main motive to write this book is our former president of India and scientist Dr. APJ Abdul Kalam, who once said that whoever has a message to sharpen their successor and spread great information does nothing wrong in writing a book.

Many stories and anecdotes are the result of a collection from numerous sources, such as newspapers, magazines, other speakers, and seminar participants over the past 25 years.

Unfortunately, sources were not always noted or available; hence, it became impractical to provide a precise acknowledgement. Regardless of the source, I wish to express my gratitude to those who may have contributed to this work, though anonymously. Every effort has been made to give credit where it is due for the material contained herein. If I have unintentionally not given credit where due, future publications will acknowledge those who bring this to my attention via e-mail: tmohammediqbal@gmail.com.

Neuro-Linguistic Programing (NLP): Introduction

Salam Alaikum! Heaven be with you. A most excellent and good day to all who read this material. My name is Mohammad Iqbal, and I am a chemical engineer. I have been in training for a long time. I have completed several programs, including Six Thinking Hats, Seven Habits of Highly Effective People, Positive Thinking, and many other personal development courses. I have also been educated in Neuro-linguistic programming (NLP), hypnotherapy, stages of meditation, and other courses. I am a Toastmaster in Arabian Toastmasters (for public speaking), a difficult, ten-module course in becoming a competent communicator. I recommend this course if your team members want to become influential. I found that getting through each step was very difficult, but (Alhamdulillah) I made it.

I have lived in the Gulf countries for 13 years working in chemical engineering, and I have around 25 years of experience in this field. You may ask why I reformed my field of expertise from chemical engineering to NLP. My motive was to enhance human performance. There are so many smarter ways to do this and so many outstanding people who need help bringing out the best in themselves. I believe everyone should reach their best capability to achieve success. My goal is to help every individual achieve a good standard of living; each person should have a comfortable, peaceful, happy, and healthy life. I feel this is vital for every individual, though some people try to do this in soul-destroying ways. Even if you want to change, it is challenging for any of us, even if we meet with therapists, psychiatrists, and psychologists.

It is hard to help a person become healthy and socially responsible, but every human has a responsibility to try to progress and grow personally. We are also part of a society. When we meet people from different cultures, especially from developing countries, we realize during those encounters that we should help the people around us. We should offer to share the experience, knowledge, and lessons that we have gained during the journey of life. I realized that I have 25 years of fulfilling engineering experience, but if I don't share this experience and the knowledge I've gained with those who follow me, what good is that knowledge?

People from more developed countries like the United States or the United Kingdom have a very systematic approach to taking care of elderly people especially on their knowledge sharing thoughts. They also provide many seminars and conferences and are willing to participate in them and share their knowledge and their expertise. Although we're not lacking in these, we need more of them, and we should gather ideas on this topic.

I had a professor who taught engineering classes in the Shanmugha College of Engineering in India who was like some professors in the United States. Basically, he was a chemical engineer and had completed two doctorates, one in the United States and one PhD abroad. When some professors have completed two or three doctorates, after 20 or 25 years of academic experience, they say, "I have gone through all the work of getting a PhD and I now have a very comfortable life. Now I want to share my knowledge and expertise with society." They find that they want to share their knowledge and experience with society so their students can perform even better. When society allows the professor to teach, it can function better. That is the professor's ultimate objective, and it is extraordinary; of course it is a good idea, and we need to adopt it. It is good to be more focused on using the talent, experience, and expertise from renowned older adults.

As I began this change of focus, I have found that I needed to overcome many fears; with work and training, I have been able to overcome stage fright and the fear of speaking to women. It took several hours of practice for me to be able to talk in front of people. Addressing a group is very difficult, but if you understand your topic and make a reasonable effort to practice your presentation, you can perform well and speak easily in front of people.

I have also completed clinical therapy with Steve G. Jones; I have studied his modules thoroughly. He is an excellent mentor and has helped me reach a high level of understanding in NLP and hypnotherapy. His insight and training along with his relaxed approach to his modules make the information easy to remember and apply. This training has been both remarkable and amazing.

That is my short introduction of myself. I am an open person, and I would like to open myself up to others so they can understand me better. I do encourage those who have questions about this "NLP for life successes" to contact me.

I wish my readers successful lives, and I am sure you will experience some degree of change in your life prospects, personal health, peace of mind, family relationships, finances, and ability to deal with fears and failures after studying NLP.

Chapter 1

The NLP Concept

NLP refers to neuro-linguistic programming. *Neuro* means connected to the nervous system. *Linguistic* refers to the language we use. The language the body uses to communicate with your nervous system is referred to as *neuro-linguistics*. A *program*, in this case, is that which stimulates your brain feedback system to activate your nervous system. Basically, it refers to the ideas and output generated by your brain.

Dr. Richard Bandler and Dr. John Grinder are some prominent people in this field. They simplified the NLP idea so that even an ordinary person could understand and absorb the essence of NLP concepts. Society is indebted to these two scholars and should remember them because we have already benefited from them for a long time.

The study of psychology began after the 18th century, and today, more people are studying human behavior, especially the evolution of the human brain and many related subjects. Scholars have put more effort into studying human origins, behaviors, and beliefs than ever before. They study many things, including depression, suppression, and anxiety, all subjects scholars began studying around 1950. Between 1950 and 1970, Dr. Bandler and Dr. Grinder were involved in their studies, showing new ways to work with human psychology. They quickly formulated these studies so NLP could benefit all people who are studying how to program their minds to improve their lives. The originators created programs to help readers achieve training at a master level, although many people can benefit from the NLP programs at lower levels of training.

The NLP concept has nothing to do with psychological diagnoses; rather, it focuses on what you think and feel during emotional reactions. NLP consists of the physical and mental reactions that occur during the following situations:

1. When you are feeling angry

2. When you are feeling comfortable

3. When you are smoking tobacco

4. When you are feeling energetic

5. When you are feeling upset

6. When you are feeling depressed

Neuro-Linguistic Programming provides many practical ways in which you can control physical and mental reactions, change the way that you think, view past events, and approach your life. It also makes you to take control of your mind, and body leading to happier and productive life.

Difference between Hypnosis and NLP

Another method for dealing with emotions is hypnosis, another scientific approach. Our brain produces of four stages of waves: alpha, beta, delta, and theta.

Delta waves produce a superior, transcendental state. Beta produces the normal state of being awake. Theta waves are in between alpha and delta waves. Alpha waves influence the brain up to 200 times the amount beta waves influence it, and many astonishing thoughts come out when you are meditating. Alpha waves create a kind of "brain dream," and many training centers are available at which alpha waves are studied during meditation and sleep to enable patients to better train their minds.

Theta waves fall between delta and alpha waves on the spectrum. Each type of wave has a different number of cycles per second: delta waves occur 3 to 6 times per second, theta waves occur 7 to 10 times per second, alpha waves occur 11 to 16 times per second, and beta waves occur 16 to 20 times per second. If you are always in an alpha cycle, you will be more able to concentrate.

It is possible to discern what state people are in. For example, people driving are often in the alpha state. Sometimes we feel as though we did not drive the entire route even though we have reached home. Similarly, when we watch television, time appears to move faster; three hours of programming occur in what seems a short time period.

This is also evident when kids are playing video games. Often, they are not distracted from the game for a long period. This state typically characterizes how people are when playing video games. These are all daily activities you can see; they make up the reasons for this study. In Hypnotherapy, we have six important steps like Pre talk, Induction, deepening, Script, Amnesia, and Trans-termination. Each step has a specific purpose in order to achieve positive programming in our minds. NLP, on the other hand, doesn't use these same steps and techniques. In a hypnotherapy session, the client is very passive while the therapist will do most of the talk; In NLP, the client is actively engaged in doing some exercises to reprogram their brain while conscious. There are advantages to both hypnosis and the NLP system. I advise you that if you have completed your NLP Practitioner certificate course, you should go to the next level and complete your Master Practitioner and Train the Trainer levels. This will give you a greater understanding of the NLP.

If you have more time, I also recommend spending at least two or three hours per week in therapy sessions, which can give you a lot of benefits, such as removing negative thoughts; overcoming phobias; and dealing with family issues, overexcitement, depression, or anxiety. Therapy can also help you tap into your subconscious mind to work through difficult emotions to make your life better. Therapy is a different approach from either NLP or hypnosis. I strongly urge you to have a mentor to guide you in learning these techniques.

Basics of NLP

NLP is a neuro-linguistic program, and communication with your nervous system is the key to unlock your potential to achieve success. The nervous system is the network of nerves from your brain down to your toes. The nervous system plays an important role in communication; practitioners call basics of NLP as the "essential" or "presupposition" of the NLP.

Presupposition of NLP

We already know that most of the brain's resources are required to achieve success. Everybody knows that to achieve success we must study thoroughly and work hard, but there are so many different formulas. Folk wisdom suggests that extra effort and more energy create more focus. Applying a neuro-linguistic program is something everyone can do, but the most important aspect is to find a catalyst, which will be seen in a person's ability to apply the NLP basics. Furthermore, every behavior is used in some context. We can say, "There are two things we will discuss if we have time," and that creates a context. All we must do is add content. Both context and content are important in every aspect of life. Suppose I scold a person, saying, "Hey, you are a donkey," and this person is my friend. I know that he knows what I mean by "donkey," but I do not want to hurt him. However, it is my language that tells him we are still friends; he made a mistake, but I am telling him in a friendly way, not in a harsh way. However, if a person who is not known to me made a mistake (such as verbally trashing my lifestyle without knowing it) and I told him he was a donkey, the content would be the same, but the context would be different.

This is NLP. We will see more examples as we go through the modules and will follow the modules with more discussion.

Ways NLP is Evident

One example is that lies can be a characteristic of poor human behavior. However, the same lies can also be used in a different approach, one that is not necessarily reprehensible. Suppose two actors perform together in a movie. They will act naturally like father and son, husband and wife, or lovers. This behavior touches the NLP in essentially the same way as if the situation were true in content (but the context is different, and it is, in fact, a lie, in a sense). We need to use proper context whenever it is applicable, but we should not ruin someone's humanity, because the human mind is a precious thing and people should not, at any cost, affect their human values.

Another method is chunking. Chunking means cutting something into small pieces; in NLP the term refers to the way people create structured, proper, and approachable ways to learn things so they can repeat the lesson in their everyday lives. If you want to finish reading a 200-page book, it is okay to try, but it may not be not possible for you to continuously read it for two or three days, and doing this may also not be beneficial to your health. Instead, what NLP teaches us is much like slicing up a book chapter by chapter, then completing it in 10 or 15 days. Every day, read a portion of the book until you complete it. Similarly, bodybuilders who want to change their body structure cannot do stretches and hundreds of push-ups and pull-ups to build up their body on the first day. Rather, they build their musculature systematically each day. They do some exercises for their abdominals, then for their arms and legs, thus building up their muscles in a structured way. When they do this, they achieve that bodybuilder structure after a time. The NLP tutors and other people who contributed to the program made it a systematic and approachable program. When it took up a longer time, they divided it into smaller portions, allowing students to learn and benefit from the concepts being presented in smaller chunks.

Another way to view a person's NLP is through their failures. Some view failure as a stepping-stone to success, but others think that failure is just a stone. The fear is of "false evidence that appears real." We should not be afraid of failure or become cynical. We should not have negative thoughts, and whenever we experience a failure in life, we should treat it as feedback. From the feedback, we try to learn many things, and because we learn, we can give that lesson to our successor. Another way of dealing with failure is always seeing the positive side in everything about the failure. Although some people see an empty glass, we should always see it as full. Some therapists today recommend not using cynical excuses like "I cannot, so I will not." Rather, we should find a way to attempt to reach a goal. Even if we don't reach that goal, we can learn from focusing on it.

Finally, according to NLP, we should build a mental capacity to see beyond the way things are supposed to be. Try to see similarities between the way you and another person view a picture, and then look at the picture from a different perspective. Then, when you look at the picture, it is actually different from either your or another person's description. We should develop the mental capacity to see beyond our own viewpoint.

These are all essential ways to view NLP. In summary, I discussed the NLP "essential," also called the presupposition of NLP, and I talked about chunking, which is dividing the more significant portions into smaller potions. I suggested we should always try to see the positive side of life, that there is no failure, and that it is important to develop our mental capacity to see beyond our limits. Each of these behaviors is useful, no matter the content and context. Finally, I discussed how people have internal resources and the only thing lacking is a catalyst. This catalyst can be evident to anyone who undergoes NLP training or watches NLP-related content.

Thank you for your attention. I believe this program will provide many benefits if you complete it, because if you only learn a portion of it, you cannot understand or implement it fully. Continue to the other sessions, and work with me on them. I welcome comments, and have provided an email address in the preface. I encourage all with questions to direct them to me. I am sure the series will be helpful; I will not discuss only theory with you but will explain using my personal experiences. For example, speaking to women and talking in front of a group were my biggest fears, but I overcame all of it because of NLP and diagnostic therapy. Hence, I want people to benefit from this chapter, so they can pass the lessons on to their successors.

Chapter 2

NLP Techniques: Introduction

Salamalaikum and good morning! Welcome back to another beautiful session. I hope that the last session have been useful to you. In this session, we will talk about the significance of NLP and procedures that can bring excellent results. There will be a question on how about NLP techniques result? The answer to that question is around 85%–90%; it has proven which is scientifically amazing.

There are three ways that people successfully implement NLP techniques:

- How we understand them and

- How we put them into practice matters most in determining the individual success of the NLP techniques.

- The effectiveness of the trainer and how he or she trains you (usually using repetition of techniques so they stick in your mind) make a difference. A good trainer with the right attitude will help students of NLP apply the techniques properly and make them effective in their daily lives. For people who already have these practical skills, taking this course allows them to achieve other success milestones.

Simply said, if you add these NLP techniques into your day-to-day activities, you will raise your energy level from the time you wake up until you go to bed. You will not feel that your energy level will be less or that you will feel less motivated to do your work, and this is the advantage of using NLP techniques.

What areas can we improve with these NLP techniques? As I have mentioned in previous recordings, everybody wants to have excellence in their life. They want a peaceful and financial abundance. They want motivation, energy, and the ability to solve their physical or financial problems. All these things need to be accomplished, simply to make life less complicated. The NLP techniques help in this area, especially in building relationships. Some people find it more difficult to meet with a customer and sell a product, so we will cover some techniques in successive modules to help with sales-related activity. This will help you achieve success in business.

Finally, some people experience phobias, negative thinking, or fears. If they adhere to the rules of NLP and are doing the exercises as the trainer has taught, they will begin to see results.

Sensory Responses

We go now to the next topic: sensory response activation from our childhood. You might have learned in elementary school that there are five senses that provide the brain with signals. These senses are so important (eyes, ears, skin, nose, and mouth) that they are called the "five essential senses." Generally, NLP uses these five senses in a productive way to enhance both performance and overall energy levels:

1. The eyes enable visual communication.

2. The ears enable auditory communication.

3. The skin allows us to feel touch.

4. The nose allows us to smell.

5. The mouth, tongue, and taste buds allow us to taste.

These five senses will be important in future sessions, so they should be remembered as one of the fundamental concepts of NLP. We are going to use these five senses to increase positivity in our lives.

We will discuss these five senses in the coming text. I will offer glimpses of techniques I have been trained in. For example, we want the responses and activation of the senses to check in with our friends, and we need to have experiences and the feeling of enacting each response regularly. We can also go back to our childhood days. There will be some pictures to use as prompts, and you will be asked to identify five or six different sensory signals in each picture.

Visual Techniques

This first technique in NLP is the visual technique. In this section I want you to imagine yourself back in elementary school and see if you can have six or seven different pictures in your head. Now ask your friend to stand in front of you and look at him or her for 10 or 15 seconds. This activity requires three people: the performer, who is being looked at; an absorber, who will look at the performer; and an evaluator. In this case, I will be the evaluator. I will ask Person A to stand or sit in front of Person B. Person A will make a gesture, and Person B will monitor Person A for a few seconds, close his or her eyes for a few seconds, then ask Person A to make a different gesture. The evaluator will now ask Person B to explain the different gestures that Person A has made. This exercise requires that Person A change the gestures a few times, and Person B will absorb, note, and respond. The evaluator will decide whether Person B's observation is perhaps correct or not. After a few repetitions (perhaps five), Person B's observation skills in NLP terms are noted and the sensory and response activation can be evaluated. The more times a person practices this exercise, the better he or she will get. For example, in our one trial of this exercise, Person B observes trees and the path they shade. We will see small changes if we practice the activation of our visual response.

Auditory Techniques

We will talk about auditory techniques using the same three-person format, in which Person A is a performer, Person B is an absorber, and Person C is the evaluator (I will again serve as the evaluator). In this scenario, we will ask Person A to produce a sound. Person B will listen to the sound and calibrate (observe through nonverbal movements) it while Person A makes the noise. Person B needs to recognize the sound. Then, Person B can ask Person A to make another noise. Person B will absorb the new noise and his or her mind will calibrate it, naming one sound for Person A and one for Person B, according to the different sounds made. For example, Person A could use clapping, whistling, or blowing. Then all they need to do is interchange the A and B sounds. You can interchange the people or sounds, or you can bring another person in to make another sound so that the moment that sound is heard, Person B can say, "This is Sound A; this is Sound B, and this is a sound from a new person." First, Person B needs to calibrate, and then he or she can tune and better activate his or her conscious mind.

Kinesthetic Techniques

Kinesthetic means connected to feeling, or related to the sense of touch. A group of three or four people is also required for this scenario. First, Person B will be the absorber again. Then ask Persons A, C, and D to touch Person B's legs or hand or some other part. Make sure the person doing the touching gives his or her name and says, "This is me touching your hand" (if they are touching the hand). Have all three people take a turn touching as Person B calibrates his or her mind on the specific location being touched (the hand or leg or giving a handshake to each other). After some time, ask Person

B to absorb the feeling, which is done by closing the eyes. Then ask the people to change positions and perform the same activity until all have had a chance to be the absorber (Person B). After a couple times, the absorber will recognize a specific handshake or a specific touch from Person A, Person C, or Person D and will be able to distinguish one from another. In that way, the activation of Person B's brain's sensory component will be enhanced and his or her response will improve.

Olfactory Techniques

Now we are discussing the olfactory sense and the nose, and the exercise has the same structure, except that the participants will use some perfume or flowers to create a smell. For example, Person A may bring a lily, which gives off a specific smell. You can take different flowers to Person B for different smells, but you must have Person B calibrate each one and absorb the smell before introducing the next one. First, Person A will allow Person B to touch the flowers while smelling them. Then Person B can say, "This smells like a rose" or "This is a lily's smell," for example. This process will enhance Person B's olfactory sense because exercising the smelling component of his or her brain will enhance his or her ability to smell.

Gustatory Techniques

The last technique is gustatory, which is related to your mouth and sense of taste. Using the same format, imagine the taste of a lemon, or keep a lemon on the table and ask Person B to visualize it. Then ask Person B to cover their eyes. In a few seconds, ask them to absorb the lemon. This will stimulate the creation of saliva in Person B's mouth. Ask Person B what their response is. Alternatively, you can give Person B an orange. We have done this exercise using a lemon but will have to try it with an orange to see if it will help Person B's creation of saliva as a specific response. Either oranges or lemons are acceptable—whichever food will make the absorber feel good and stimulate the secretion of saliva.

To recap what we discussed today, I began by discussing the importance of NLP in our day-to-day life. We noted how it provides results and what areas NLP influences in people's lives. We also talked about sensory responses and practicing quicker and more accurate activation using the five senses.

Thank you very much!

Chapter 3

Approaches

The experiences that we have in our minds play an essential role in providing useful insight into the problems we are handling. Furthermore, the brain takes the information from all of the five senses (seeing, smelling, hearing, kinesthetic, and gustatory). From these five sensory systems, which make up the representing system, our brain processes information through submodalities. Moreover, stimuli affect the brain, and in some cases, the reaction will be stored there. Furthermore, when the reaction is stored, the experience that causes it creates a specific and repeated response each time it occurs. It can be an internal force or external behavior that brings this result.

Moreover, regarding the approaches to the behavior modeling that we got from Person B's responses, we need to analyze these approaches to discover how to produce a quicker or more accurate response to sensory stimuli. If the results are not very good, then we need to replace what didn't work with another method and other techniques that provide a better result. This is also called *denial,* and in NLP, it is also called *modeling.* This term comes from the work of G. A. Miller, E. Galanter, and K. H. Pribram (1970). Also, it is available in their book, *Plans and Structure of Behavior.* In behavior modeling work, the authors have discussed the models that one may possess. We will test this behavior and analyze the outcome of this test in their model, which they call a door model, or the "test operate, test exit" model (Miller et al., 1970); you can see this process is tough, but it produces good outcomes. Moreover, we need to have specific questions to deal with correctly, from finding a love to understanding a book or solving a family issue. To have a complete good understanding of this sort of submodality, you need to master this representational system to have the right approach for the issues and problems that we want to address.

Timelines

NLP uses a timeline to tackle negative emotions such as anger or bad behavior. We will use the example of some body losing their business to demonstrate the timeline therapy technique.

First, there are two concepts: *in time* and *through time*.

- In time, your body is moving away from the axis of the past and future.

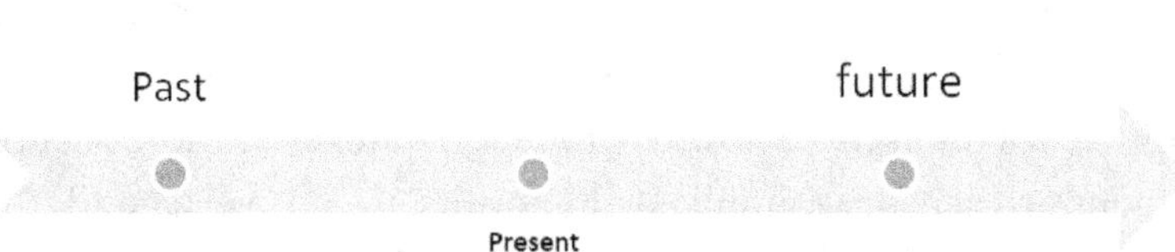

- Through time, your body is moving along the axis of the future and past.

This is the representational system of the way timelines work.

1. Some people will physically represent past and present time. For example, the past will be on their left side and the future will be on their right side.

2. Similarly, some people imagine the past as physically behind them or on their backs and the future as before them or on the fronts of their bodies.

3. Some people will have this occur diagonally in opposite directions for past and future timelines.

Now imagine the client feels the loss of a business deeply, and they need to fix it using a timeline NLP technique. That person would need to float back (meaning mentally take themselves back in time). They need to move from their present sad mindset. It would be best if they floated back in time, perhaps to before the time of the incident, maybe two years before losing the business. The person would mentally form a picture or series of pictures of symbols associated with a business loss.

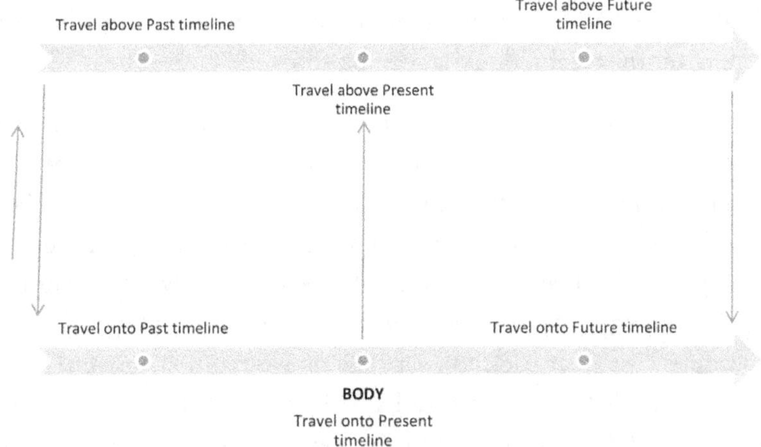

Another way would be to approach the business above the timelines. Just imagine time as a line just above some point. It would help if you used all the sub modular stimuli to visualize the picture, and it would be best if you flowed around the timelines. Now we need to check the person's emotion and ask them to distance themselves from their current emotional state and learn from it. If you feel negative behavior coming to your mind, say to yourself; let it go, smoothly and effortlessly without much attention. You need to concentrate on just the positive lessons that come from the experience.

Check to see whether the person can recollect any positive knowledge from the exercise. After this step, have the person travel in the past to that period of time. It would help if you used the same submodality to influence each exercise, like the loss of the business and the emotions that come from that incident. Ask what lessons were learned from the loss of the business. Then, have the person mentally travel back to that period of time for a while. Have them remember the situation and then move back to their present condition. By doing this with the present condition, the person performing this technique will ultimately release the negative energy with the result that the picture should be very detailed. Only then can you release the negative emotion. Some people have difficulty creating the visualization. For those who do not have good visualization abilities, there is another technique that can be adopted.

For this exercise, the person needs to move from their present condition and travel to the future. In the future, maybe the person would have released all the negative energy. Ask the person to check the submodality stimulus and then go along the axis of the future, floating on it and then waiting until they completely release all the negative energy. Do the test one more time, repeating the same procedure. Just float back to past time above the past timelines and on the past timelines. Then float back above the past timelines to the present timeline. Finally, float again above the future timelines and on the axis on the future timelines. Then we need to get back above the timelines, floating back to the present condition, meaning that we need to travel back to the present. By doing this exercise, the timeline technique will ultimately help a person release all negative energy.

Chapter 4

Strategies, Patterns, and Approach

There are many moments in life where we use an approach in a particular way to deal with a problem and deal with the activities that we will do every day. We play the "take a specific approach for a specific result" card. Sometimes this is called a strategy, even for things like buying material from a shop, expressing love, or other moderate problem-solving or decision-making tasks. All these are affected by the specific way we approach life and issues. Is the question now how to deal with the activity or the issues associated with the activity?

First, we need to have good knowledge about dealing with family issues. Second, we need to have the skills that are required to deal with the situation. Third, we need to determine the best attitude toward or approach to that problem. If we miss any one of these, it will be difficult to make a correct choice, and the outcome will be different.

If your mind is properly tuned, it will be easier for you to approach any problem. For this approach, the participants' minds have been influenced, and this will produce a specific result. Suppose I am buying material from a shop. Perhaps it is a grocery shop or pharmaceutical store. Asking the vendor about the purchase requires a specific question. If you want to shape the outcome, you need to shape your approach. If you are changing your approach, you need to have some other model in mind, and you need to rehearse it and store it in your brain. Then you can execute the new action from memory.

As far as NLP is concerned, the output can be changed. Why should it not? If you change the approach correctly, the outcome will also change. This can be adopted in different stages and approaches. We need to see the results to get the outcome we want.

Purchasing/Selling

For example, say you want to purchase a car, and you are arguing for a discount on accessories you want. If you are determined and have a plan in your mind, you will have a set of specific questions that will enable this seller to reduce the price, reduce the installment, give some concession, or add some accessories. So, this outcome will produce a good result.

You need to test this method. If it produces a good result, then use the same kind of strategy for other things. Similarly, this technique can be used to sell products. For example, a salesperson incorporates a particular lead that sets a specific set of constraints on ways of answering the customer. In this process, customers have many questions in mind about the product or its advantages. You can minimize the disadvantages of the product and learn how to convince customers to buy it. You can learn to sell the product at a higher price to make a profit. This method has been tested and produced improved results.

So, if a product is available at its best quality and the salesperson has a specific way of selling their product, they can change that approach to be more effective. When salespeople see that the outcome is good, they can adopt this specific approach and achieve sales success. We can see its effects on sales and strategies of selling and strategies of buying.

Learning

Some people like to read in the early morning. Some people like to read in the evening after 8:00. There are different kinds of approaches to learning. According to their output and according to their potential, when they feel relaxed, people feel comfortable studying and absorbing the learning material. So, they form a specific time and mental approach to learning that provides a good result.

Suppose some people wake up at 4:00 a.m. and don't eat anything. They start reading for two hours, closing the door and leaving only a small window open so they can breathe fresh air. This is their preferred learning strategy. On the other hand, some people study by increasing their voice and eye modulation, reading very quickly, and memorizing material. Similarly, some people read in the evening after 7:00. These people prefer night studies. So, there are many approaches to learning, but we need to test whether a particular form provides better results. Suppose I am reading in the afternoon but not remembering content, and I am reading only five pages in two hours. What happens if I change my approach to the evening method? This kind of testing needs to happen to determine the best learning technique for an individual.

Decision Making

We have talked about openness to new knowledge, skills, and attitudes. It is helpful to write down all the positive and negative views of probable outcomes. Then, out of these outcomes, we need to rank each of these decisions that the person is making. We can then look at specific approaches to each decision. A person can also change their approach if the result is not what they expected. The individual can then make a refined list, bring new values and new kinds of information to the decision-making process, and then reevaluate.

Self-Motivation

Some people have a specific approach to self-motivation. Suppose they are very depressed and feel a lot of anger. They use a specific approach to change those feelings. The change causes them to have low energy. In this case, NLP can tell us how to increase our energy or balance our energy and control that anger. We need to have our own approach to NLP to make it successful, so it will help us be more self-motivating.

Problem Solving

First, we need to define the problem. Then, we need to find the associated factors and facts for these problems, including the extenuating circumstances and date. Suppose too many events are happening in the same weekend?

One survey states that the number of accidents goes up on the weekends. One of the Gulf countries has used its accident statistics to create effective strategies. The government now cautions people to take extra precautions (following lanes, restricting speed, keeping adequate distance between cars) over the weekends. First, we need to find out how we can avoid accident-associated issues. We need to test this approach; if it is not effective, we need to adopt a different approach. Then, we need to research expert opinions, if possible, for inclusion if needed.

This approach can be used to overcome a smoking habit, kick an overeating habit, and find a partner, so we can use an approach specific to the problem. Then, we can test it, and if it does not work, we can try again to find one that gives the best result. If a method is not producing a good result, we can modify our approach so we can use it.

Chapter 5

Vision, Mission, Belief

Let's talk about vision and mission statements. Companies have vision and mission statements, and their main purpose is to describe what they want the company to achieve in the future. All the employees of this company want to achieve success. Suppose you are working in the cement industry, and the company wants to be an industry pioneer for the next two decades. This is their vision.

Fulfilling the mission statement will mean providing employment, education, and training to local people. These details will be included in the mission statement. The main purpose of the vision statement, then, is to display a broad view of the company's destination and the direction the company needs to go. This is what the vision and the mission statement will do for the company and for its personnel.

You can also make a personal vision and mission statement that provide focused information on the purpose and the destination you want to achieve. You could be building a house or for achieving financial independence, but a personal vision and mission statement is stronger than one for any task.

Creating a personal vision and mission statement will be great for encouraging knowledge sharing. You can write a statement that assumes that people want to share knowledge from their many years of experience. This experience from many years of training can be focused on the people you come across. For example, my target audience is middle-class people. I could create the goal of helping other people. I also have a goal to help 200 people get an engineering degree. Other people might want to help people become financially independent.

For this exercise, the goal is to achieve financial independence. Making this statement will clarify in my mind that this is the goal I want to achieve. I need to read it frequently. It is also helpful to display it prominently in a room, like your living room or bedroom, preferably by a mirror where you can see your statement and see a reflection of your face. You simply display your statement and read it once or twice a day. You can reframe it as you read. As you have different kinds of thoughts and experiences with this statement in mind, you can redefine and reframe to improve on it. You want the statement to be a flexible one so it will help you to achieve success.

Similarly, the personal mission statement can be applied to your family. Perhaps you want to provide education, knowledge, and skills for your children. A sample family mission statement could look like this:

- I want to provide a good, sturdy atmosphere for my children.

- I want to be financially independent.

- I want to face my life with principals of give and take, with flexibility, not with rigidity.

Statements like those above can be used to analyze a value. Believe all those things and understand that it will take time. It's not simple. These are just some samples for guidance, so you need to explore the details yourself. What do you actually want to achieve in five or ten years? What kind of life do you want? You can put your answers in a step-by-step statement. This will help you to achieve success in your life and avoid the troubles that happen during life. Specifically, if someone ever wanted to divert you from your purpose, this statement could help you stay focused.

Here's an example. Let's say you want a job abroad. Then you would of course, after reading about job vacancies in newspapers, change you mission statement. This statement would provide you with direction, although you could change it. It doesn't matter if it changes. It will still give you clear guidance. I am not right for the business world because I already have experience in that area and that experience was not helping me. So, this is my motto. This is my mission:I will provide free lectures to many people. Can you see how a statement like this will keep you from drifting away from your purpose? And that is how a vision and mission statement can help.

These are some people who did not have a written vision and mission statement. People without a written vision and mission statement cannot achieve any success. Only 5 percent, or five people from the sample, hadmission and vision statements. They had a good clarity of mind and purpose because they were studying, which is a kind of focused job, and they have been successful.

Logical Level Model

The logical level model was developed by Robert de Leeds and inspired by the work of Gregory Bateson. This is a neurological level model that is also called a logical model. It is structured from bottom to top like a pyramid:

1. Spirituality

2. Identity

3. Value

4. Belief

5. Capability

6. Behavior

7. Environment

The above stated seven items are important because they all pertain to human behavior; the human mind works with all these things. If your environment is good, then you have good values, good capability, and good behavior. If the environment is bad, there will be bad results and less desirable outcomes. Everything we might desire changes the technique you would use to change you or your environment, to change your behavior, to adopt a new capability, or to acquire new beliefs and values. All these things can be done with NLP. Therefore, in this model, these elements are all interdependent.

If you want to make one change in the structure, that will affect the entire structure of the pyramid. Suppose you want to change your behavior; you believe that will affect your capability, behavior, and language. But behavior is at the bottom, like changing the environment. It is not easy to do this. It takes effort and energy. So, given this setup, we will first talk about the details of belief.

Belief

Belief is deeply conceived and embellished thought that is programmed in one's mind for either success or failure, good or bad. Interestingly, people are more likely to believe that something is false and that failures indicate truths about people. This is found to be true in both the conscious and unconscious mind. Sometimes we come across certain incidents in the newspaper or on a video that we consume unconsciously because they go directly to our subconscious mind. Whenever a strange incident happens that is not like real life, our mind recalls these situations. If that situation is conceived as bad or as a failure, then we remember it as a failed one. Either these deep-rooted experiences stay with us or we have absorbed others' experiences and we have absolved ourselves. However, we are still storing them in our brains.

Opinion and Formed Facts

A fact is a statement that can be verified. It can be proven to be true or false through objective evidence. An opinion is a statement that expresses a feeling, an attitude, a value judgment, or a belief. It is a statement that is neither true nor false.

There are many opinions, and some have become like facts over time. We know there are differences of opinion, but we adopt the collective opinion. From the majority opinion, we see the big picture. The opinion we present to others is stronger because it is built out of a successful time-tested model. We need to analyze the facts and make a judgment. They will determine whether the results are good or bad. This is the belief system that is adopted in our brain. NLP provides you with the means to change your belief from bad to good.

Let's talk about another example. Suppose a person is laid off from a job but is positive about the situation. They believe they can find some other job. Or maybe this situation makes them realize their value and potential. Let's hope and believe that this person will gain from their experience and knowledge. They will find a better job than the old one. All they need to do is frame that thought, and they can have a positive belief about how to think about the situation. In this case, the person analyzes all the financial implications and other aspects. But because those are not under his or her control, except for looking for the ultimate job, there is no reason to worry.

Conversely, if people have negative feelings, if they think that the job they lost is the only job they can do, that it is the end of their career, and that their life is ruined, these are completely useless and negative thoughts. A person cannot succeed in this life if they have these kinds of negative thoughts. They need to make a move toward positive thinking. They also need to move forward in applying for a job. They need to find their skills and talents and look for a solution to have some sort of job so they can make a living.

Now, in the second example, we will focus on family issues, especially divorce scenarios; many people view these scenarios from a negative perspective. Perhaps the wife and children left, and she took your hard-earned assets and cheated on you. That can make a person more brutal and less productive because the mind is occupied with thoughts of these failures. These are tough issues with many negative results. Even if the spouse is in the wrong, one can control negative feelings. You may think, "They used to respect me as a father," or, "I worked hard, and when my father was alive, I took care of him very well." This attitude might be called "old-fashioned" or "antiquated"—these ideas that have persisted throughout the 20th century about our parents will not help us to move forward. This is part of a negative perspective.

If you think there could also be a positive way to think about something this bad, you are right; lots of people have to deal with similar situations. Women have the right to leave a marriage. After all, this is their life. It is important to respect peoples' feelings and values. In this vein, there was a real-life incident that happened in the UK. A married couple and their daughter immigrated to the UK from India. They had a loving marriage and had been living together happily for eight years, and they had a beautiful daughter. However, after many years of living together, people's likes and interests will change. Their personal goals and objectives might differ. Spending time with different peer groups or friends could alter their whole thought processes differently. In this example, the woman believed that she was wasting her life and energy in taking care of a man who was not worthwhile. Of course, that man was honest, a workaholic, and good-looking, but she believed differently. She now felt that he was not as capable, talented, or impressive as she was.

Some people have experienced negative situations in their lives. Despite that, they help to sustain their family lives and help their spouses through such a situation. Negative implications are a part of life. We are all brought up in different ways. In the example above, the situation continued for three or four years and became intolerable. The daughter was ten years old. During the separation process, the father was attached to the daughter, and he was angry because her mother got custody. It appears that repeated violent thoughts overwhelmed the husband, and in a fit of anger and frustration, he killed his ex-wife. The court put him in jail. Now, the daughter, who saw this incident, and the daughter was traumatized. Fortunately, the daughter had relatives who adopted her.

The point is that we need to respect the values of the system in which we live. If you don't have control over negative thoughts, things can go badly. You will be stuck reliving negative implications and could need psychiatric help, or you might want to kill the other person, an extreme case. We are not in a neutral position. So, the point here is that we must respect others' feelings. We need to give other peoples' priorities importance. Of course, everybody has the right to decide whether to continue in a relationship with the same person or not. Let us follow the laws that are given to us. But if you do as this man did and succumb to a fit of anger, things change. All three people involved are now in different situations: one is dead, one is in jail, and one has lost her parents. We do not know how she will grow up. We do not know how many years her father will be in jail.

If you are positive, you believe that life will give you another chance. Maybe I will get another good life. I've seen people who have married and failed many times, who still love life and are focused on living happily at an older age. There are lots of opportunities out there. We just need to build the habit of positive thinking in our minds. We need to be able to plant the positive seed in our minds to overcome this kind of difficulty.

Beliefs That Become Habits

Now we will discuss examples of beliefs that become habits. What you believe becomes a habit, so you need to be vigilant about what you believe. Sometimes things you see unconsciously become beliefs. Unconscious beliefs are thinking arrangements we have in our mind that we have no attentiveness to what we are presuming. They are formed early in our life, either through a strong emotional event or through restrained replication. An example of it is, "I am a total failure, so there's no point in attempting any new thing." These often lead to issues, such as whenever issues come to your mental and emotional surface and take actions based on that.

There is an old story about an elephant and its trainer. The elephant trainer, called a *mahout*, said that when he was training the elephant, they tied the elephant baby with a small rope around one leg. This was a very strong rope that the baby elephant could not break. So when the elephant grew and became much heavier, it would still be tied with the same kind of rope, even though it could break the rope easily. The animal is controlled by its thought process, which was programmed by the mahout when it was young. So the elephant, from its childhood, kept the idea in its mind that it could not move because it was tied with the rope, which is the training model. The point here is how conditioning with this rope allows the elephant to be controlled.

Another story is about a washerman and a donkey. When the donkey was young, the washerman used to lift it and carry it into the water on his back for fun. Then the donkey grew. One day, the donkey fell and could not get up. So the washerman thought he would try to carry the donkey to another village. He believed that because he could carry the donkey when it was young, he was used to it. So he tried it, and he was able to carry the donkey. The point here is that the training you undertake will help you to do things you might otherwise think you could not do.

A third example is about the placebo effect. As you know, some people always think they are sick and that they need to see their doctor and take some medication to get better. Some doctors understand the placebo effect and know that their patient doesn't have a fever, cough, or other symptoms. The doctors used to give only medicines like multivitamins and minerals, just those that were also proven effective in psychology studies[refer for further reading to Luana Colloca's *Neurobiology of the Placebo Effect, Part I* (2018) and *Neurobiology of the Placebo Effect, Part II* (2018)].

The word placebo was used in a medicinal context in the late 18[th]century to describe a "commonplace method or medicine," and in 1811 it was defined as "any medicine adapted more to please than to benefit the patient." Although this definition contained a derogatory, it did not necessarily imply that the remedy had no effect. It was recognized in the 18th and 19th centuries that drugs or remedies often worked best while they were still new, and this practice had good results. The magic of this medicine, although it only consisted of vitamins and minerals, was that it worked. Furthermore, patients thought that just by visiting and speaking to the doctor they would become comfortable and their diseases would be cured. There are many examples of people with illnesses, troubles, and issues, either physical or mental, whose willpower and strong minds enable them to overcome actual physical diseases or mitigate their symptoms.

It is also good to discover that inventors have strong beliefs about their work. For example, Henry Ford was strongly determined that he would invent the compact modified V-engine that would run a car. He was successful with all his efforts and energy. In doing the research and development into building this engine, he finally could succeed. Similarly, Thomas Edison, the inventor of the light bulb, talked about his hundreds of failures. His achievement came from his determined faith and belief in his mind. In his quotes, Edison says that being a genius doesn't mean that you are necessarily an intelligent person. He said that the most important thing is perspiration, and that comes from hard work. Sometimes achieving something doesn't take any intelligence, good ideas or brilliance: "Genius is 1percent inspiration and 99 percent perspiration. I have not failed. I've just found 10,000 ways that won't work. Our greatest weakness lies in giving up. The most certain way to succeed is always to try just one more time."

The Wright brothers invented the airplane. Wilbur and Orville Wright said, "It is possible to fly without motors, but not without knowledge and skill." They also said, "The desire to fly is an idea handed down to us by our ancestors who… looked enviously on the birds soaring freely through space… on the infinite highway of the air." Wilbur and Orville Wright were American inventors and pioneers of aviation. In 1903 the Wright brothers achieved the first powered, sustained, and controlled airplane flight, and they surpassed their own milestone two years later when they built and flew the first fully practical airplane. The brothers had been tinkering with the idea of flight off and on since childhood. They were mechanically inclined young men who were inspired by the efforts of others.

These beliefs are sometimes wrongly programmed from childhood days, such as when teachers misguide us. Suppose a classroom has 30 children in it; the children cannot be taught on a fast track. The teacher cannot give the lower-performing children enough attention. Some even tell them they don't see how they will prosper in life—they are told they will be big failures. Teachers have to have strong minds to resist making negative impacts. Otherwise, failure will be programmed in children's minds, making it impossible for them to prosper or advance, which is why the number ranking system in some of the schools has been changed to grades. Studies may not determine good performance or help people in actual life. That is why they always say that practical experience is different from being in school. If they scold and keep repeating negative feedback, some teachers may unintentionally program children with negative thoughts. If you are not aware of the programming, then your life will show all the negative impacts. The point here is to hold on to your positive thoughts and release all the negative energy and thoughts to go to the next level.

How to Change Beliefs

Now we will talk about how to change beliefs. There are many techniques available in NLP using visual, auditory, kinesthetic, olfactory, and gustatory submodalities. The submodalities will be the color, contrast, and brightness of the actual moment. If it is a sound, you have pitch, oscillation, and intensity. All of these things are submodalities. We will use them to change a belief from negative to positive. First, we need to identify the belief, which is not a simple task. It will take quiet time. You need to sit in a comfortable, quiet place and write down all the positives. What is your goal? What do you want to be? What you want to achieve in life? Then, determine whether you have written positive or negative beliefs.

Positive Moments

Have you determined whether you have a positive belief? For example, suppose you believe that you are successful and you want this successful belief model. To keep it, you will talk to yourself about happier moments. There are two moments from my own schooling perspective on which I draw: at Sixth Standard, I got the General Proficiencies (overall total marks for that year), which is valuable. I still remember walking across a big stage to receive the award from the school principal. It was very moving, and it was one of my dreams. I had achieved success by proving general proficiency in Sixth Standard. So, I can recollect this successful belief model. I have included all the submodular stimuli, like what kind of uniform I had on, what kind of food I ate that day, and how I walked. I remember what kind of sandals I wore, and how I moved across the floor and then walked the steps of the stage on the right side when my name was called. I shook hands with my principal. Then I received the certificate, and I felt very happy. The second incident occurred when I was studying in Tenth standard. I scored 99 marks out of 100 in Math and 99 marks out of 100 in Science. When I saw those grades, I felt proud and happy. My teacher clapped and told me, "You got wonderful marks." It was one of the best moments of my life.

Both moments are successful belief models to use as an example for your own benefit. You can reframe these kinds of positive, happy, and successful beliefs to work in your own life. Everybody will eventually have some kind of success; even a smaller award works. I believe that at some point in time, each person has felt appreciation. Appreciation moments are equal to thousands of happy moments. Furthermore, appreciation is so much stronger when you recollect it that can be truly emotional.

Take the happiest positive moment and frame it in your mind as a big picture. We talk about the rituals with all the colored brightness, and we play on the submodality that I just talked about. We need to take our own time in doing this exercise.

Negative Moments

Now we need to think about negative moments and then learn to shift the negativityin our minds. Some possible scenarios are as follows:

- I'm not getting promoted in the organization.

- My wife doesn't understand me and always finds fault with me.

- My children are angry with me for no reason.

- I feel I am a total failure.

These are negative thinking patterns. Whenever you have a negative moment, **frame it in your mind as a small picture, and put it in black and white**. Don't give color to this image. You also need to keep it in the corner of a happy moment that is a larger picture. Frame the negative thought picture in black and white and reduce it to a smaller size, like a passport-size photograph, and make the happier picture much larger than the negative picture. Focus on the negative thought in the small picture, and finally let it diminish into a tiny dot. Repeat this exercise four or five times, and it will give you a good feeling as you pass through your negative thoughts.

I have personally done this experiment many times, and it has been effective. This is one of many beautiful techniques that NLP has given us to help us recover from the effects of negative programming and negative thoughts and become successful people.

Chapter 6

Rapport

We always think of getting good feedback from other people. Everybody wants to share their views with others, whether they are right or wrong. Everybody also wants to achieve success by building rapport with others, like taking extra workload from others or by convincing people to buy a product or idea to get a promotion or monetary benefit. Building rapport is a powerful technique that allows us to understand how to create connections with people, even if it is with children, a spouse, or family members.

Some people say that nobody will stop my older brother when he talks. Furthermore, he builds rapport. He builds a feeling of respect and of a good self-image. Moreover, he makes everybody want to understand him; I have even seen some family members try to emulate him. Some think my younger sister is like a princess with a crown. They listen to her. She talks about many facts, gives excellent guidance, to be successful in adopting her methodology. This is the image that people build by creating rapport with people. It is a form of charisma that you make part of your personality. Similarly, a good teacher builds great rapport with his or her students. Furthermore, when a student passes from one grade to another, the teachers feel very proud and happy. Connection with students is evidence of the rapport built by the teacher. It is powerful. Furthermore, it is binding because it strengthens the association between student and teacher.

There are many instances that show how building rapport helps us. Sometimes, when you are attending a party, it is likely that two or three people in that group grab the attention of all the other people. The way they speak and present themselves and the energy they project are mesmerizing. In fact, these highly motivated and chatty people can convince anybody of anything. They keep talking and motivating others, making the entire party joyful. This is another example of building rapport. We have also talked about building rapport with yourself on an unconscious level, using NLP.

The following passage comes from the *Definitive Book of Body Language* by Allan and Barbara Pease (2004).

As far as the technical study of body language goes, perhaps the most influential pre-twentieth-century work was Charles Darwin's The Expression of the Emotions in Man and Animals published in 1872.

This spawned the modern studies of facial expressions and body language and many of Darwin's ideas and observations have since been validated by modern researchers around the world. Since that time, researchers have noted and recorded almost one million nonverbal cues and signals. Albert Mehrabian found that the total impact of a message is about 7 per cent verbal (words only) and 38 per cent vocal (including tone of voice, inflection and other sounds) and 55 per cent non-verbal. Professor Birdwhistell made some similar estimates of the amount of non-verbal communication that takes place amongst humans. He estimated that the average person actually speaks words for a total of about ten or eleven minutes a day and that the average sentence takes only about 2.5 seconds.

Like Mehrabian, he found that the verbal component of a face-to-face conversation is less than 35 percent and that over 65 percent of communication is done nonverbally.

Body Language

▨ Verbal

▨ Non Verbal
  Facial Expression, Tone of voice, movement, apperanace,eye contact, gesture, Postures

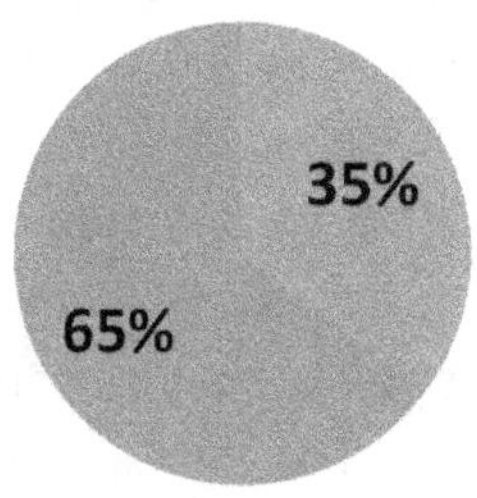

Voice Modulation

Voice modulation is important, especially when we are giving a presentation or a speech. The tone, speed, and transitions we make from one sentence to another are significant.

The Words We Use

Similarly, the words we use at the beginning of a speech and the conclusion are important. The way we adopt these elements for public speaking plays an important role in building rapport with the audience so the audience can understand the message we want to convey.

Body Gestures

Another tool for building rapport is your body language, or your gestures. The way you project yourself with body language reveals and conceals things about you. In fact, underlying all your body language are clues about the message you may be delivering in your speech. Body language is very important for building rapport between the audience and the speaker; it is even applicable during phone conversations. These things are important in accomplishing the task of building rapport. What is the lesson you want to convey?

Further, sometimes we use unnecessarily high-pitched voices and inappropriate body gestures that might cause others to think we are not good. I realize that I behave like this. It is subconsciously programmed into all minds, but we need to eliminate it and talk about how to overcome unconscious judgment. We should not be judgmental, especially when we are having discussions and when we are accepting instruction. We should control our body language and our voice modulation, which is specific in nature. It can hurt people, or it can convey a message differently. So, you should try to get in the habit of enhancing your body language and voice modulation, so your nonverbal language matches your speech.

As I mentioned earlier, the beginning and end of a message is important for all instruction. The nonverbal systems, body language and voice modulation, are more effective than the verbal component of a face-to-face conversation.

Communication cannot be based on nonverbal systems only, however, especially communication that is writing-based, like letters or email. But when you want to give oral instruction, your voice modulation needs to be well executed. It plays an essential role in holding peoples' attention and conveying your message.

Mirror Imaging

In body language, one technique is called mirror imaging. This technique is implemented by making a mirror image of another person. Suppose a person uses their hands and makes gestures. We need to observe their gestures and make our own gestures the same way. This helps build rapport with another person. Suppose one person frequently uses a specific hand gesture to express his thoughts. To show we understand, we can use the same gesture.

Mirroring a speaker's gestures will help build rapport with that person. Other expressions may include nodding, exhaling strongly, and matching the other person's eye blinks. You might mirror a person subconsciously, building rapport with them and conveying the message that you are aligned with each other. It is like mimicry of thought, which also builds rapport and helps your conversation continue. Moreover, the rapport that is built can make you feel more comfortable the next time you talk.

Mismatching

Another way to build rapport is to mismatch body language. Perhaps you want to try to control a situation by adopting a person's approach and body language. If you match someone's body language, that person may want to dominate. He or she will consciously change their position because they do not want to have congruent body language with you. If rapport is not the goal, the other person will surely behave like this. We find this in very rare cases, but "they do exist, according to body-language experts." Most of the time, people are consciously aware that they are mismatching body language and have a purpose. When you mirror a person and they do the opposite, you can bet they are intentionally mismatching. I believe that this happens only on rare occasions.

Chapter 7

Reframing

In this section, we are going to talk about reframing. Reframing means framing our thoughts, opinions, and ideas differently so we have a better understanding of how to improve. There is a saying that we need to look at the positive aspects of life—this is a form of reframing—because life is a trade-off between the good and the bad. If we want to spend a lot of time at work to earn a million dollars, which may lead to a more comfortable life, we will surely lose some part of our personal life. We might need to sacrifice family time to achieve success. Nevertheless, this is a work–life protocol. We need to understand that we have only one life and need to find a balance between our work and our personal lives.

We can reframe almost every aspect of our lives in positive ways. For example, suppose we have a glass filled with liquid. People who are pessimistic (negative thinkers) believe the glass is half-empty, whereas people who are optimistic (positive thinkers) believe the glass is half-full. This shows different perspectives on things depending on the way we frame our ideas, thoughts, and opinions.

We might use inappropriate words with our children or our friends. For example, if I call my friend "stupid" when I am angry, I do not really mean my friend is stupid, as in slow-thinking—I called my friend "stupid" because I was angry with them. If my friend misinterprets the statement, it could seem that I am being abusive. But if my friend understands my meaning and my emotion and can reframe the contextual background of my anger, then my friend would not scold me for this. It may be that in my background there is something someone has done that makes me react with anger. My friend could then conclude that that is why I used the word "stupid."

There are two types of reframing: context reframing and content reframing. Context reframing relates to the situation in which something takes place. We reframe when we look at something and change it—or our perspective—so that it is in a new and different context. Content reframing refers to the details of a situation or problem. Using both types of reframing in our lives, as when we change jobs can be as simple as writing down all the positives and all the negatives. You can give each positive and each negative a score between one and five and evaluate. Writing down the positives and negatives will give you different perspectives on the situation. You can then evaluate all the positives and the negatives you see in both your current job and the new job, including comfort level, monetary benefit, and educational level, so you have a balanced perspective.

If you practice reframing and look at both jobs, they each have their own positives and negatives. For example, say a new job pays about 10 percent more than the old job. However, the new job will be in a new environment, and we do not know what the workload will be. We might need to move our family, including older adults who may live with us, so we need to consider their comfort levels. Furthermore, suppose the older adults are being treated at a particular hospital by a particular doctor: How will you manage the care relationship? You need to systematically evaluate the positives with the negatives and balance the two. If you successfully reframe the negatives of both jobs, considering context and content, then the negatives become positives, and you might not need to shift from your current job to the new job.

Reframing content works in this situation. Sometimes by doing this exercise—writing down positive and negative details—the answer will tell you what is causing your dissatisfaction with the job or with the current situation. Reframing helps you examine your feelings so you can discover a more positive frame of mind. You don't need to worry, and you don't need to go for the next job you are looking for.

There are similar cases, such as when a person looks only at the negative aspects of a spouse or has only negative expectations of them. We should not look at only one side of a person or one aspect of their character. There are also the good parts of a person, and we need to come to an understanding of why someone may be struggling. Perhaps they are working to give us a comfortable life. We would like this activity, even if their temperament is bad. Sometimes it is still okay, and we can live with them with the proper compassion. If we can encourage them to receive some personal counseling to reframe their negative temperament, we can build on our interpersonal relationship. Reframing can change life decisions that we want to make, whether it is separating or taking a new job.

We can use the tool of reframing multiple scenarios in our personal lives to help us develop a better, more positive perspective of life.

Anchors

In this session we are going to talk about anchors. Whether in a small fishing boat or a large steamship, proper anchoring in the seabed will prevent a ship from running aground. In high winds, an anchored boat will stay in position and not be shifted here and there.

A picture, touch, smell, or sound could be considered an anchor. Now let's talk about how to incorporate this anchoring idea. It's a kind of touch therapy. You touch and make an anchor and attempt to tap your subconscious potential to produce the best version of yourself.

Negative energies will turn positive if you do this repeatedly with proper timing. The behavioral changes you want will be achieved quickly, and you will replace the negative thinking with positive thinking. It's an intense and rewarding experience, accessible through the anchoring technique. Anchors are external stimuli, or touch or triggering points, that provide internal responses

Many of our daily behaviors come from the anchors we are used to thinking about. Some people are preoccupied with negative thinking, while others project positivity. For the anchoring technique, we need to have in mind the sensory systems we discussed previously on the visual, auditory, kinesthetic, olfactory, and gustatory (VAKOG) technique.

The first system is visual. When you see an old school picture, you may immediately reconnect your thoughts to childhood memories. We can use this picture to improve ourselves, converting childhood memories into positive results now and in the future.

The second system is auditory. When you hear an ambulance, something fearful may come to mind. The siren sound is stressful. Similarly, when somebody knocks on your door at night, you might picture a thief or an intruder.

The third system is kinesthetic. Imagine the feeling of getting promotions, higher grades, joining a dream job, or recalling some happy occasion. Any of these can trigger certain memories or feelings.

The fourth system is olfactory. We might smell someone's cooking or perfume and recall someone we used to know, for example.

The last system is gustatory. The taste of certain foods might cause you to recall a loved one and stimulate your mind.

In this anchoring process, we can tap the subconscious to produce positive results. Psychologists have analyzed the responses of dogs eating meat while music is playing. They have shown that playing the music before feeding can cause the dogs to salivate. They have adopted the same stimulus approach to influence human behavior.

Innate responses and feelings are very important for anchoring. However, anchoring can sometimes fail if you have a poor visualization through a submodality response. If your response is strong enough and associated with positive emotions, the anchoring will be productive.

An anchor can be set—or it can be fired off. We can cause an anchor to be removed, either consciously or unconsciously.

Nested Loop Anchors

"Nested loop anchors are stories that bypass the conscious mind and access the unconscious mind more easily. It is a trance-creating method used to bring a reader along with the characters in a story." (Dr Richard)

Nested looping here refers to a storytelling technique. Can you find a way to engage an audience and get their attention while selling valuable products? In this case, the products would be our ideas and messages. Nested loop anchors can help a storyteller grab people's attention and mesmerize them; they will think unconsciously about what is being discussed.

You might see this with movies. After one scene, viewers may make a decision about the characters' future actions. What happens in the next scene? The audience will create a new story that fascinates them, and the nested loop anchors will cause them to think subconsciously. What about the previous scenario? What is going to happen? The audience keeps unconsciously thinking about it. They will either accept it or, more unconsciously, they will find a solution by thinking about it. What will happen to scenario one and scenario two? So the audience will combine the multiple stories and multiple chapters in their heads. This creates five states for the audience: anticipation and attention, gaining information, curiosity, creating, and wanting to know more on an unconscious level. This nested looping will provide you with the kind of audience "cells" to which you can market your ideas. Marketing strategy benefits from using nested loop anchors.

Chaining Anchors

Chaining Anchors practice of chain of emotional states anchored in sequences that can make people move into a positive state without being coerced. The overall goal of this exercise is to help people control anger and stop procrastinating suing.

The mind's conditioning can trigger a response, as experimented by the Russian scientist & Physiologist Ivan Pavlov with the dog, the piece of meat, and the music.

While playing music, he gave the dog a piece of meat and watched its response. The researcher repeated this test, and when the dog ate the meat, it secreted saliva. After repeating this scenario, when the researcher removed the meat and only played the music, the dog would still salivate. This conditioning principle is used to modulate peoples' anchor by creating a trigger that can create a response. Using touch to condition a client to move from procrastination to motivation in the way Pavlov used meat and music to make a dog salivate. We will discuss how this training and practice can make people move into a positive state without being coerced. The overall goal of this exercise is to help people control anger and stop procrastinating. In 1903 Pavlov more fully explained the findings, at the 14th International Medical Congress in Madrid, where he read a paper titled, The Experimental Psychology and Psychopathology of Animals.

The example that we will use is arranging the books on bookshelves. These can be labeled using various categories from the book titles. First, we are at the procrastination stage. Then we move to the frustration stage, then to positive energizing adjacent states.

Finally, we move to the motivation state, which can be extremely high for some. We will use the hand if you are working with a client. You can use your full fingers to initiate touch on the client's knuckle. The connection between the hand finger touch and the movement makes a person from one un-resourceful emotional state to resourceful emotional state.

Procrastination state → Frustration state → Energizing state → Motivation state

1. First, identify the state that you do not want to feel. In the book arranging case, our reaction to the arrangement of books on the bookshelves is that state. Procrastination state(right hand forefinger will touch left hand forefinger knuckle, to have anchor1

2. After identifying the feeling, we need to add a sub-modality: the visual, kinesthetic, auditory, or gustatory stimulus. We need to feel that impulse. Stimulate test and calibrate (check) the state.

3. Second, Frustration state we need to use right hand middle finger will touch left hand middle finger knuckle, to have anchor 2. This is to overcome from the laziness obstructing you to move to next state.

4. Break the state between each of them, stimulate, test and calibrate (check) the state. Make sure it is properly anchored (anchor2).

5. Third, Energizing state we need to use right hand Ring finger will touch left hand Ring finger knuckle, to have anchor3). This is to move away from the frustration state.

6. Break the state between each of them, stimulate, test and calibrate (check) the state. Make sure it is properly anchored (anchor3).

7. Four, Motivation state we need to use right hand small finger will touch left hand small finger knuckle, to have anchor4. This is feel extreme passion, extremely good feeling we need to have to attain rearrange the book shelf in our example.

8. Break the state between each of them, stimulate, test and calibrate (check) the state. Make sure it is properly anchored (anchor4), break this state. This is the essentially to be tested in all, four states.

9. Now fire anchor1 as you reach peak of state hold down anchor1 and fire the anchor2

10. Release the anchor1 and hold anchor2

11. As it reaches peak state, fire anchor2 and while holding anchor3.

12. as you reach peak of state Release the anchor3 and hold anchor4

13. Break the state from anchor4.

14. Repeat the whole chaining processes same way three to four times.

15. By doing this chaining anchor the procrastination will get changed to motivates state. In future pace, if we come across some procrastination we can do this same anchoring technique that helps to overcome.

If you are working with a client, ask them to think of a frustrating moment with a sub-modality giving a little more color and fewer feelings, less contrast and color.

In this exercise, you still plan to have extreme, delighted moments, motivating moments, extreme feelings of passion, and to find the client's comfort zone while organizing and arranging the books on the bookshelves. You feel extremely motivated.

We will use the knuckle and the four fingers, one by one, to touch and release. Finally, we will come to the fourth knuckle and we are released from the first state. So, this is a method for turning procrastination away. When we achieve a peak experience, break this connection, which is the second finger with the other knuckle. Ask the person to return to the frustrated state. Then, when they feel very frustrated, have the person release it.

Take second finger, and then press the third finger on the third knuckle. Ask the person to check the modalities when they are at peak release. The individual releasing frustration does this when the fourth finger is touched. This is the motivation state.

Then you release the fourth finger from the fourth knuckle. Now you have completed the training and have released the anger or frustration. We will repeat the same steps for three to four times. Then we do a firing of each state as planned, which is the first finger with the first knuckle to start the procrastination state. This is a firing-off state.(Firing an anchor – Repeating a behavior that triggers a certain response).

The individual will feel they will have fewer feelings of procrastination because we have done the anchor training. They then find that Chaining anchor eliminates them lethargic, and then they move straight to a motivated state.

Resources Anchors

Now we will discuss a type of resource anchor.

1. The step is to recall a positive event more confident, happiest and motivated State.

2. Break the state between each of them, stimulate, test and calibrate (check) the state.

3. Make sure it is properly anchored (anchor1), ANCHOR it with a touch of arm (right)

4. Break this state.

5. This is the essentially to be tested

6. We need to identify the behavior that you want to improve. The anchor you have in mind can be a touch, picture, smell, or sound. (anchor2), Anchor it with a touch of your other (left) arm.

7. Next, Integrate and combine anchor1 and anchor2 to get the resourceful effects

8. Take this resource (anchor2) and relive that unsourceful behavior (anchor1), Watch and listen to everything that happens as those two experiences combine. It will be even more effective.

9. This is the essentially to be tested in all, two anchors.

10. Fire anchor1 and look for a new response.

11. In future pace, if we come across some negative feeling in the past we can do this same anchoring technique that helps to overcome.

12. Now, stop thinking about it for around thirty seconds. I prefer a thirty to forty seconds maximum.

13. The last step is to make it right until we get to the peak feeling. If we don't get the anchor right, there could be something wrong. By applying the stimulus, do we get a particular feeling?

Now we will go to another example of the same kind of resource anchor.

1. We need to decide on their positive state, and we need to incorporate a strong feeling and a strong response using VAKOG.

2. We need to recollect the same feeling. Please note that if you are going to perform it for your clients or anyone else understand their feeling reflected properly,

3. Next, select the anchor. I usually prefer touch.

4. You can use a three-finger touch on the wrist, or whatever you prefer.

5. Anchoring more than one state with different scenarios is also possible.

6. But we need to allow sufficient time between the first and second anchor.

7. Then we need to test the anchor.

8. Imagine having the same experience and feeling when touching and keeping the anchor.

9. If you don't, you need to find another more positive feeling to overcome the negative thoughts.

Collapse Anchors

It is similar to a resource anchor, replacing a negative anchor in NLP with a positive one for the same stimulus. Used for when a person or client repetitively goes into a state (not for beliefs) that they wish they didn't go into and don't seem to know how to get out of it. Anchor the new emotion and amplify to ensure that it has the force and that the client can easily return to this state. Collapse and Integrate When ready, break state, activate both anchors simultaneously, keeping a close eye on the client's reactions.

1. We need one positive anchor and one negative anchor.

2. A positive anchor, we need to decide on their positive state, and we need to incorporate a strong feeling and a strong response using VAKOG.

3. A negative anchor is a negative feeling that we want to eliminate.

4. Then, after this two-anchor fix, use the same hand on a different side.

5. After that, we need to touch and break state of each other to neutralize or collapse this negative state.

Circle of Confidence

There is a circle of confidence, imagining you are driving a BMW or Mercedes-Benz when you are driving a normal car. This is the kind of confidence we need. We need to imagine driving a Ferrari.

Furthermore, we cannot know everything about every subject. During an interview, maybe you can express 80 percent of your capability or maybe only 60 or 70 percent. In that case, you would not perform well. However, if you were writing your responses, you might get up to 95 percent. Confidence expressed through body language and the way you modulate your speech will convey that you know a lot about a subject. You are confident in yourself, you want to join the organization, and you want to succeed. Moreover, you need to work out some lagging things and reset your mind and then analyze your delivery in the interview to bolster your confidence.

It is important to rehearse extensively so the interview will be easy, both from your perspective and the interviewer's. You may want to enroll in some seminars on how to interview. You might want to try to give a confident presentation to an audience of 100to 200 people when you are preparing.

Self-confidence is essential in presentations. Rehearse in front of a friend or close associate, or record yourself on a video or audio recorder to see how you perform.

Confidence applies to any situation in which you want to perform well. Sometimes we may feel nervous about speaking in a new environment or on a new stage. But there is a mental trick you can use. Lie down on the floor and imagine presenting to 500 people on an ideal stage. Mentally walk through your speech and the PowerPoint slides once or twice. Keep a notebook handy so you can write down corrections or hints for improvement. This technique works very well.

Many scientists and even Nobel Prize winners attribute their successes to mental rehearsal and receiving feedback from the subconscious. In many cases mental rehearsal is important toreachingthe circle of confidence. If you are an athlete, you can mentally rehearse to improve your performance. In NLP we talk about the circle of confidence, and if you imagine this or any other scenario on stage, you could even be rewarded as a student in the classroom as your classmates applaud and your teacher praises your performance.

You can bring to mind any grades, college experiences, or hard work you did when others appreciated you. Just remember the incidents and put them on the imaginary stage. Think about a time when you won a medal, or when a professor appreciated you, shook your hand, and touched your shoulder. Remember all those feelings, and run through them until the picture is vivid, seeing your friends and other students witnessing your happiness and confidence level.

Just imagine taking a picture of that moment in your mind and putting one anchor in your hand, like putting a good sign symbol on your finger. This is what exceptional circumstances and perfect output are like; keep this image in your mind for 30to 40seconds and then slowly release it.

Whenever you lack confidence, just practice like this and you will feel your confidence building. If you are not feeling confident, try rehearsing by imagining a time you received appreciation in front of a group of people. Doing so will help you achieve the circle of confidence.

Parts Integration Technique

This is another type of integrated technique. As you know, integration means combining two or more resourceful states. Suppose we want to do two activities, such as physical exercise or watching TV. It takes one part of the thinking do some physical exercises and the other part of the thinking to watch the TV show.

For example, say you are questioning whether to watch the TV show or go to the gym. The kind of result you desire is good, but you are in conflict: you want to go to the gym and work out, but you also want to relax and watch a TV show. This can make the mind confused. In the end, the activity that has a higher priority and higher motivation for you will gain more attention. If your attention and motivation are not directed toward the gym to work out, naturally you will tend to relax. Your attention is focused on these two scenarios. One will strengthen your body and mind. The other one is due to you—you feel you've earned the right to rest. This creates a kind of conflict between two opposing motivations.

We can integrate these parts into the parts integration technique. First, you consider, "Tomorrow I will go to the gym." You can even postpone "tomorrow" to a later day. This is the sequence: the event and the scheduling need to be taken care of without conflicts. Once these conflicts are resolved, then you will have good motivation for doing the job. You lose interest in the behavior of relaxing too much or watching TV ends.

I prefer, for the anchoring, that you hold your fingers together, touching your hands on your thigh, using all the submodalities we've discussed.

Consider what kinds of thoughts are coming to mind and what kinds of submodalities are activated: the visual, auditory, kinesthetic, and other sensory input. Then break this state and look at it. Now, you will be triggered with resourceful behavior, or good, positive behavior.

Then take the anchorout. Let's look at this anchor. Now look at the one with the resourceful behavior—good, positive behavior like exercising in a gym. So let's trigger that behavior.

Using your right leg and right hand, holding your fingers together, touch your hands on your thigh.

Relax and anchor with a deep submodality all over. This will be a positive and resourceful behavior. Remove your finger from this state after 10 to 30 seconds.

Do anchoring for the unresourceful state, with the unwanted behavior of relaxing too much or watching TV. You should end up on your left leg; your left hand will be holding your fingers together and touching your hands on your thigh.

What do you do next? Now hold both of your hands out, and play simultaneously, with both the legs and both hands, the resourceful anchor and the unresourceful anchor. Let us feel all the submodalities. We can feel the energy flowing, and it allows the submodalities to integrate.

After you do this for 20 to 30 seconds, you fire off the anchor. Then, take your hands off your body. We can feel the energy flowing, and it allows the emotions to integrate. You will see the effects and energy levels rise, for one is under resourced and the other was resourceful. If you repeat this process, you will feel like you have more energy.

Chapter 8

Filters

In this section, we are going to talk about filters. The filters are a hypothetical. The filters of the NLP Communication Model are Meta Programs, Belief Systems, Values, Decisions, and Memories. Meta-Programs: The first of these NLP filters is Meta Programs. Knowing someone's Meta Programs can help you clearly and closely predict people's states, and therefore predict their actions and behaviors.

Example of it your speech affects the way people think about you. If you say everything people do not like, you'll lose the trust of anyone. Friends won't trust you with their important secrets, if you do not preserve and keep it in filter before you will turn to someone else to share information they don't want everyone to know.

You can see it. The guard is a frame of radiations. You can see a frame of film that you filter in your imagination. And you can put it like a pyramid. You can put it as a circle across you. You can put it in a square ora shape you want to adopt differently. But I would like to see you take the pyramid. The pyramid structure is a very strong structure. So, in the case of a negative thought, imagine this pyramid, the structure, the guard, and the film form of the radiation. Imagine that the pyramid structure is put like a gate on your body to protect you from negative impacts.

Several years ago, I had taken many of the trainings, and one of my coaches told me about the importance of these filters. They work, and I have been using them whenever I encounter bad incidents or accidents because these things are a part of our life. But the negative impact should not have any consequences in our subconscious and conscious mind. That is the purpose of this kind of imaginary filter.

The negative thoughts arise from the unwanted treatment you receive, which goes into your mind. I call this a personal protective guard (PPG), and it will help us a lot. Similarly, in companies, PPE stands for personal protective equipment, like goggles, gloves, earplugs, and safety shoes. So you can call this a PPG that will protect you from all this negative impact we are directly involved in or see in front of us through electronic media or by direct experience. Life will not always give us a positive outlook. Sometimes we experience deaths, accidents, or other incidents.

So our mind should not receive the bad impact of these negative occurrences, and they should not be conceived by our consciousness. That is a basic thing. So in using this imaginary filter, you should imagine you are inside a pyramid. The pyramid structure is put like a guard on your body.

The pyramid is made up of radiation film that protects you from negative impact. Imagine you see an accident in front of you. Just imagine that. Close your eyes for 20 to 30 seconds. That makes a conscious filter so that blood coming from a person, their crying, or the collision's impact should not affect you. We are human; it is good to have feelings and emotions. But the person who is badly injured will make an impact on the subconscious mind.

Sometimes, there are electronic media of different resolutions and pictures with colors and combinations of sounds. These media should not affect the person who is grieving; many say it affects our mental health. So this kind of filter will help us overcome negative impact. That is, we are always either reading or consuming thoughts or listening to somebody elaborating in a particular way or seeing things with our own eyes. If you come across negative issues, use this kind of filter; close your eyes for some seconds and put on this filter. This will help you to overcome these negative effects.

Energy Bouncers

I want to talk about energy bouncers. There are several energy bouncing techniques in NLP. We'll start with energy balance and energy bouncer techniques.

Wake-up Energy Call

When you wake up in the morning, just grab two fingers. Then put your hand on the top of your head and give a soft massage to your body from the right and then over your head to your shoulder, then descending to your abdomen, then to your thighs, then to your feet.

If you do this two or three times, your energy will be balanced across your body, and you will feel refreshed. You will feel so much power and strength. Every time you wake up, apart from your religious thoughts, just imagine that this day is for you, and you are born to win. You will win today, and you will get all the prosperity, the wealth, and the support you need to achieve your accomplishments today.

Start with that. I bet you will have a wonderful day.

Energy Tapping Exercise

There are seven important points in our body, and we need to tap this energy. This is the exercise you need when you have low energy. We want to have more energy and more confidence. There are some places in your body where you have glands: on your head, forehead, below your nose, then your throat, then your navel, then the last four inches below your navel.

You just put your two fingers in these spots and just use some sort of vibration for five to tenseconds. See the picture for the energy activation points.

So if you keep working with these points, you will have highly activated energy flowing across your body.

Locking and Unlocking Energy Exercise

I will now give you another locking and unlocking energy exercise. When you are stressed, when you have a lack of oxygen in your body, this will help you. However, let me elaborate. See the picture below.

1. Cross your hands.

2. Move your hands together toward your chest.

3. Tilt and bring your hands to your front.

4. Tighten up, inhale slowly as you count to five, and exhale slowly as you count to ten.

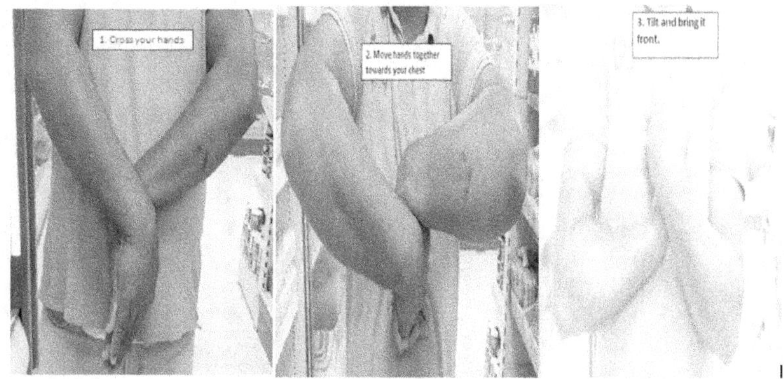

Based on your breathing in and out capacity this count doesn't matter. But just inhale deeply and exhale slowly. That will help you relax your muscles and get the energy required for your body and brain.

There is also a way to relax your attention if you are working on something for a long time. You want to just recite some words in a different language without knowing their meaning, like *Yoyo aguna matta tataa.* This is a different language; you will not know the meaning of these words. Saying them will help you change from the subject you are reading to another subject.

Hand-Waving Technique

Another technique is called a hand-waving technique. Wave your hand up and down four, five, six times. If you want to get energy, you need to go from down to up, toward your nose, four or five times. Suppose somebody is coming at you angrily. Don't let a full fight develop, and then he will be calmed down. Give him the energy; just bring your hand up four times.

Chapter 9

Energy Bust-Out Exercises

Sometimes you will be angry. This is bottled-up emotion, and we want to let it ventilate out. Suppose somebody scolds you and behaves badly. This is also an imaginary exercise. Imagine that you have put it in a red-hot balloon or whatever form you want. Still, you give it the color visualization moment, all of the vigor, olfactory, and gustatory things in your mind. Then you poke a nail in it and it all busts out. Do this for a few seconds; this burst will relieve all this negative impact.

So to summarize, in this chapter, we discussed the following:

- The energy boom technique

- How you need to have a range of energies when you wake up

- The eight important gland points that need to be tapped

- Locking and unlocking

- Hand waving.

- Energy-boosting when a person was having a bad impact on you

Answering a Phone Call

There is one more technique for answering a phone call when you are stressed or when you are focused on something and somebody calls. Let the phone ring and count from one to five or five to one. This action will calm you down.

Then you can speak to the person who wants to contact you. Remember that you already have PPG with positive radiation. I prefer for this pyramid to have a very strong and unbreakable structure to help you overcome any negative impact that will affect your mind and your body.

Enhancing Easy Learning

In this section, we are going to talk about enhancing easy learning. Sometimes we want to learn a new subject, such as chemistry. Some people are allergic to chemistry and chemical reactions.

In NLP, there are techniques that make it easy, so a person can like a subject. It is also an anchoring technique. We can also apply it to learning new things, new subjects, and new languages. For example, I am allergic to chemistry; I am more interested in English literature. So I will anchor the feeling in the same hand in two different locations. We need to associate it with all the VAKOG submodalities.

On your hand, the difficult subject should be at an elevated position physically, and the easier subject should be at a lower one. So we need to tap on this, and we need to touch under the difficult subject. Imagine the difficult subject touching on your left hand side, and access the modality associated with it. You feel that this subject is hard to learn.

Then we relocate after a 30-second gap related to an anchor. You put on the low side the easier subject. You can also apply the submodality and all your feeling. As with previous subjects, we need to intensify the feelings so that this anchor will be strong.

Then we need to do cross-mapping with both anchors, the difficult one and the easy one. If you do that, alternatively the difficult one and easy one, it will neutralize the effect of the difficult subject. The hard subject will become an easy subject.

Sometimes people who don't like a certain subject can use these small techniques in their life to help them understand the subject. They could be very good in the subject after changing the learning state so that there are two other factors: liking and disliking.

Suppose we are studying math and the teacher is not teaching properly or we have a bad feeling about them. Then we have a mental block. We restrict ourselves not to read or understand if it has come from teacher X, but if the same subject is taught by teacher Y and our mental picture is that Y teacher is terrific, we have a great interest in whatever teacher Y is telling us. This will help us gain knowledge more easily.

But in NLP, we dissociate from the image of the person. Suppose we cannot understand something, butwe don't form a negative image of the teacher and the subject. We dissociate from it. We like to get good marks, so we concentrate on the subject and focus on the learning.

Negative states can be changed for ourselves also, and they can be changed for the people we are interacting with.

We have already talked about diverting people's mind states. By changing someone's position or changing his thinking and eye moment, we change, too.

Chapter 10

Eye Cues: Attachments and Detachments

We are now going to talk about using a moment to understand a person's behavior and the sensory data we talked about in the previous sections, such as visual, auditory and kinesthetic. And there is another type: internal dialog. For example, if someone is making an upward movement on the right hand side, that is visual data.

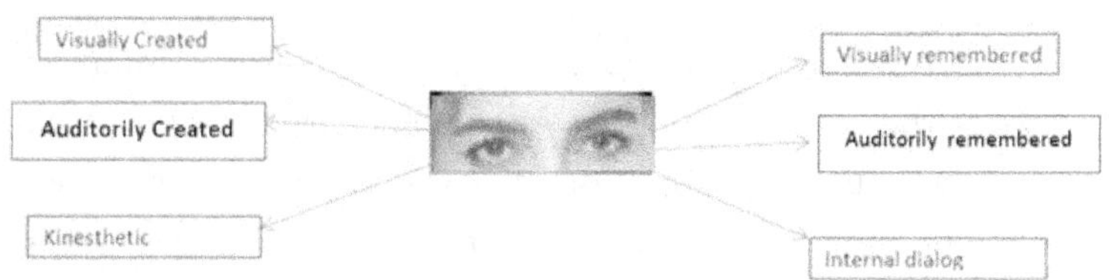

If her eye movement goes down on right side, it is kinesthetic. If she does it on the left eye side, it is an internal dialogue. So, internal dialogue is when she is thinking too much, and she wants to recollect from her memory.

If she is either creating something in her mind or constructing something from her thoughts and artificially conveying the information, and if she moves on her left side, you can see that these were recollections from actual memory.

These are the two simple things that help you determine if one is constructing a thought or recollecting from memory and giving us the information. However, we need to calibrate this behavior before we determine a person's behavior by ourselves. Now during the calibration, we need to ask the person if we can first ask another person about one year before now.

"One year ago, how was his life?"Ask someone the question and watch the behavior pattern of his eyes. And if he is visual, then his eye movement should go naturally to a higher elevation.

And if he is constructing a statement, then they will go to his left hand side, if he's recollecting from his mind, and if he is constructing something artificially, they will move to his right hand side.

You can understand how this is going to help us. So now another question. You can ask the person, what does your car sound like? What is your mobile ringtone? If he is an auditory person, his eyes will stay in the middle.

Can all these exercises be done with a person not interested in disclosing the information? If some people are adamant and don't want to give you any information, they will be silent. And sometimes you can see them close their eyes if they don't want to discuss the subject with you anymore.

For NLP, this is a technique for understanding a person's behavior, and I would like to give some more information about the visual person. If you ask them a question, they think of it as a picture, and they will give a quick reply. Mostly they are organized, and they are always color-oriented.

Auditory people listen a lot, and they speak a lot. This is a peculiar characteristic of the auditory people. And they always have a human touch with people. They are very close because they will always look for the improvement of the their family members, and their friends. They will speak in a low tone, and they speak very slowly. They always have the human touch.

The other one is internal dialogue. It's a mixture of visual, auditory, and kinesthetic data.

Now, we will discuss why eye movement is required; it is just to understand the person—he's calm and composed; if he's having negative thinking or is upset, we can find out.

And sometimes we know if we are tense. And if you have too much pressure, eye movement will be rapid. If you are sad and depressed, your eye movement will be downward, taking a look at the kinesthetic area.

So you can understand it in that way. And sometimes when we are thinking, we stare at the walls of the room, thinking meticulously on issues and problems. This way, you can tell the person in this state.

However, this is all only the surface. It's not the only determining factor that governs the person's character. It's just a basic glimpse of a person's behavior. And we should not practice these ideas on our loved ones, which will create unnecessary issues in our family.

For example, if your wife is coming from the office and there's a pattern change, and we cannot simply conclude that she is coming from a friend's house; she may have gone to her relatives' home, or the children may have acted similarly. Likewise, if children tell lies and we catch them, we should understand that we should not take it as conclusive, because children are children. But in NLP, this is a technique for understanding a person's behavior.

Some studies say the husband and wife have different patterns; the husband is always a kinesthetic person, and the wife is always an auditory person. But there will be mismatches. Suppose the wife likes to talk a lot and the husband wants to keep himself calm and composed. They may have a lot of differences of opinion in this situation. However, this is not the only factor determining the relationship.

It is essential that the NLP practitioner and master practitioner understand that the basic behavior of the human being is based on eye moment and the idea of giving you information on how a personality works using eye clues.

Next, we will talk about the state of mind. There are different ways to understand your mind state. Some people say "I'm not in a good mood" and others say "I'm in a good mood."States vary from person to person.

There are two kinds of states: attachment and detachment.

So what I would like you to do is think of the most important event you enjoyed in the last ten years. Or take three or four events and plot it against the years, exploring your feelings, including your visual, auditory, kinesthetic, and internal dialogue feelings.

What is the feeling you have when you are feeling success in those moments?

Similarly, make the same graph for when you are sad, depressed, or looking for help.

But the number of events that you enjoyed in your life should be higher than the number of events in which you were depressed. Plotted like this, it may seem that there are five good events and three bad events.

But it is better to keep the bad events and numbers less than the good.

In the association state, what we do is in the attachment state. We tend to feel the actual victory, the happiness of that due to circumstances that we come across. Now I want you to imagine the actual moment when you close your eyes.

For example, imagine there was an appointment you received from a big company five years ago. That was a very happy moment. A billion people could get a job like this and not feel that moment. What were the sounds, the feelings, and the colors you experienced?

On the other hand, imagine a sad moment, view the fewest number colors and give it the least importance. Don't bring everything into the surface of your heart. Just bring a small portion of this small incident, a small portion of the sad movement. Make it feel very, very dull.

The moments that are happy will become more prominent. After some time, the dissociation will gradually decrease in your mind, and it will get rid of your negative feelings.

So this exercise will help you overcome this experience of sadness, the experience of failures, and all those bad incidents. The thing is, you need to make the picture very dull so you don't give more importance to a picture of a sad moment.

Instead, with pictures of the happy and joyful moments, give them more color and more movement in your mind. It will help you shift from negative thinking to positive thinking and get rid of all your past sad moments.

Learning State

Suppose we want to learn some new language. How do we learn? The learning state of mind is very simple. If you want to learn a new thing, just close your eyes and start counting one to five in ascending or descending order. If you tell yourself that you will learn easily, you will learn quickly and comfortably and get all the resources you want to learn.

Keep repeating this counting three or four times to calm your mind. Then you start reading, and then you start understanding the subject. If you have a mood swing or some sad event, you cannot learn as quickly. So you need to calm your state.

You need to go to the learning state and get rid of all negative feelings. Then you start reading and learning much more easily and quickly.

Above all, you need to defeat this issue by telling yourself, *I can easily learn this technique, and I am comfortable learning this.*

Similarly, recall all the negative feelings that you had, but with less color and contrast. And if you keep remembering these incidents after some time, you will see that you are more positive, and this negative image and the negative state will keep going away.

We can change the behavior of other negative people and also other negative states, just by changing the topic a person is speaking about and asking them to divert their minds.

I suppose, if a person is walking, then ask him to sit. If he is looking at you, ask him to look at the window, or look at the natural scenery. And if he's standing, ask him to sit. And here is another good technique. Ask him to elevate his eye moment, but instead of downward, at a different angle.

On the visual side, this will help a person go from a negative state to a positive state, but it will take some time. But if you keep practicing it, you can get a person to change from a negative state to a positive state.

Chapter 11

Fear: Movie Theater Projector Booth Technique

In this section, we will talk about how fear is false evidence that appears as real, which sometimes people call *phobia*. Normally, people who practice NLP, unless you are diagnosed by qualified doctors like psychologists or psychotherapists, will not use the word phobia because it needs to be used by medical professionals.

For example, I dread touching electrical goods because I had a terrific electric shock when I was in the Seventh Standard. So let me explain how I overcame this electrical shock with an NLP technique called the movie theater projector booth technique. This technique is widely used. I use it for myself, and on many occasions, it has produced excellent results.

Now, let's go to the need to get rid of a negative and fearful response, making it a positive one. We will do the movie theater projector exercise now.

First, we need to recall the fear. In my case, I have a fear of touching electrical wires and cables; I get sweaty. Sometimes I get emotionally upset when I recall things that happened in the past. Now, we need to break out of these emotions. Then we need to establish a resourceful anchor.

We need to put the resource anchor in it. I prefer putting it on the left shoulder, keeping a resource, and saying "confident" or "success," whatever word makes you satisfied in that particular moment. Now we need to go to the projector booth. From the projector booth, you are operating the scene from the projector booth, where they run the film and see the movie on the projector and the big screen.

First, to reduce the impact of these emotional issues coming from this negative impact or bad experience that we had, let's assume it's the electrical shock in my case.

As a projector operator, you operate the movie from the projector scene, and let's start with my case on the big screen. I took a bath with a wet towel and got water drops on my hand. My body was still wet, and then I went near the tape recorder.

Then I touched the electrical cord for the tape recorder.

Then, suddenly, there was the darkest fume coming from my right hand. And I was terrified of the shock. It was intensified, and the light flashed quickly. The shock threw me a distance from the electrical circuit. Then I see my middle finger and forefinger were partially burned with carbon deposits on them.

I unplugged the cord, rushed to my mother, and told her about the incident. She immediately put some ointment on it and told me not to worry much. She said, "But when you are dealing with electrical goods, be careful next time, especially after taking a bath. Don't experiment—first get good knowledge and experience with electrical things."

I had that fear for many years, and it wasn't easy to explain it.

We run this scenario on the projector as we describe it. It goes well, and I gained confidence when my mother told me never to experiment with the electrical goods unless I have a thorough knowledge of them, and I shouldn't touch an electrical appliance with a wet cloth.

I made this movie black and white because I don't want it to have too much emotion. Now, I dissociate and change positions.

Now watch from the audience seats—watch the movie from beginning to end. Now you will feel it should be black and white. I know when my mother gave me confidence that helped me to overcome this electrical shock.

Again, do disassociate from beginning to end from the projector booth and come back to the audience chair. Then you watch, the movie from beginning to end and quickly and safely.

After two or three attempts, then you make it with color and make it run fast. Don't make the movie go slowly. Make it quick, and let repeat four or five times from start to end where you get the confidence. You can change it to your requirements.

Suppose you have a fear of a cockroach or lizards. You can overcome the fear with the Swish technique that will be also detailed in the coming section.

So you rehearse it in the movie theater projector booth model. Then you will see the fear is gone at some point in time.

So, I will repeat the steps. First, I told my case of electrical shock from start to end. Then we need to rehearse it from the projector. Go to the audience seats; see it, and then freeze. This was a scenario last seen in the confidence building my mother gave me. You can repeat the film from the beginning.

If this does not work out in your case, I would apply the Swish pattern very well. You will make a big frame for the confident picture and the small frame for the negative thoughts.

So, combining all three techniques—resource anchors, the projectable movie technique, and the Swish pattern—will help you to overcome a fearful situation. And we need to test this often in the future to see what will come from the negative impact of the old scenario.

Chapter 12

Gather Information for Nominalization

To get the proper gathering of the information, we need to ask the proper questions. The best results are the best answers from the other person to help in this process of getting good information.

There are four ways to get information in the proper way using the NLP techniques.

1. Deletion

2. Lack of Reference

3. Unspecified word

4. Nominalization

We will detail these one by one.

Deletion

The brain processes information every moment, and at the same time, it deletes that which is not relevant to us or benefitting us.

- Just like the computer has the delete button, our mind internally removes all this information that has flown in either by visual data or by hearing it from other sources.

- For example, a person playing a video game or watching television sometimes will neglect people's voices or a phone call.

- How we can recover or restore the information that we deleted?

- For example, if you say, "I don't like that person," the NLP response is, "Why, What don't you like?" I don't understand that person. This is another example. The NLP response is, "Whom specifically you don't understand, these moral constraints, specifically about What & Whom, we are looking on the deletion technique.

Lack of Reference

This is a kind of generalization that stems from neglecting details, the "who, what, why," example of it.

- "No one likes me." The NLP response is "Who doesn't like you?"

- "They are difficult to handle." The response is, "Who is difficult to handle?"

- "They are headstrong and don't agree with my views." The NLP reply is, "Who are they? Why don't they agree with you?"

Unspecified Verbs

In this situation, there is unspecified information, or just two or three pieces of information, but the person who is having the conversation will not give the correct picture.

For example, you may say, "My wife hurt me badly." The NLP response: "What is the meaning of hurt? Is it physical, or is it mental?"

Nominalization

Nominalization is to transform a verb, but not a normal verb.

A Nominalization in NLP is a word which pretends to be a noun but is not tangible; in other words you could not place your hand on communication, or a relationship, but these words are used as if they are nouns and hard real 'things'. It can be a verb or another process word that has been formed into an abstract noun.

In NLP Nominalization is a verb, representing a process, which turned into a noun or an event or a concept. This is something that is more easily dealt with as a verb/process, than a noun/event.

Decision is for deciding. Happiness is to become Happy, Observation is Observing

- For example: The ongoing issue, ongoing hatred, will be a part of the nominal session."

- But another example is "the ongoing desk" or "ongoing monkey."

- It does not make any sense, so this will not be our nominalization.

- Another example, we can say "Life is boring." So the response will be, "How does life bore you?" Nouns inflation also; they are not normal nouns like a person, place, or thing.

- We need to check the words that fit into that synthetic frame, and then you understand nominalization.

- For example, we cannot accommodate a man who can't understand what it all is meant for.

- The trolley is not meant for carrying a person; it is meant for carrying goods.

- Saying "I regret my bad decision" is an example; the response is, "Say anything, stop choosingthis action."

- "I want a servant." The response is, "What specific attributes do you want for the servant?"

Godiva Chocolate Pattern

In this section, we are going to talk about the Godiva chocolate pattern, which comes from Dr. Richard Bandler.

1. First, we need to identify a vivid picture of something we like with all the submodality associated with this. We need to use the anchor technique. This will be a liking state.

2. Then we need to break this state.

3. We need to go to another state, like we are lazy about doing paperwork. So in the second anchor, we need to disassociate something we need to do, meaning we are always lazy, not fulfilling paperwork, and so on. So this is anchor two.

4. In the next step, we need to activate both anchor one and anchor two. With the 30 seconds of the submodular and intense feeling that we have, we need to hold both anchors simultaneously.

5. We need to repeat and see the effect of balancing across both the anchors. It will help us in overcoming the laziness, procrastination, in doing certain jobs.

Swish Pattern

1. The Swish Pattern is an NLP technique that will be used to change a person's behavior. Suppose a person is a smoker or has nail-biting habit. With this kind of habit, if he wants to get rid of it, this technique will be very useful for him.

2. First, they need to identify which bad habit to eliminate (e.g., smoking).

3. It would help if he dissociated the picture of himself. It would help if he visualized with all the submodalities required for imagining this picture—the bigger picture, the better.

4. You want to get rid of this, so you need to make a picture of him smoking, large and colorful.

5. After a few seconds, you need to make another picture in the mind by closing the eyes.

6. The best behavior is the desired state of behavior where he is confident and successful.

7. So now you have two pictures in mind, and one is the bad picture.

8. I imagine it is a big, framed photo of a bad picture.

9. And another one is a good frame with a good picture.

10. So in the next step you need to make the bad picture into a small one, shrinking and shrinking. It becomes submerged and becomes a dot in the picture's desired state, confident, the good looking and successful picture that we need to bring out. We need to protect it with all the submodalities associated with it.

11. Now, we need to switch this pattern, say six or seven times.

12. Then we need to test this.

13. Eventually, after some time, we will understand that the bad picture is shrinking and becomes a dot. Projected picture two, which was with the good character and the successful picture, will come to the front of the mind.

14. If you have bad habits, we need to test this frequently to have this continue to be with the new, good picture.

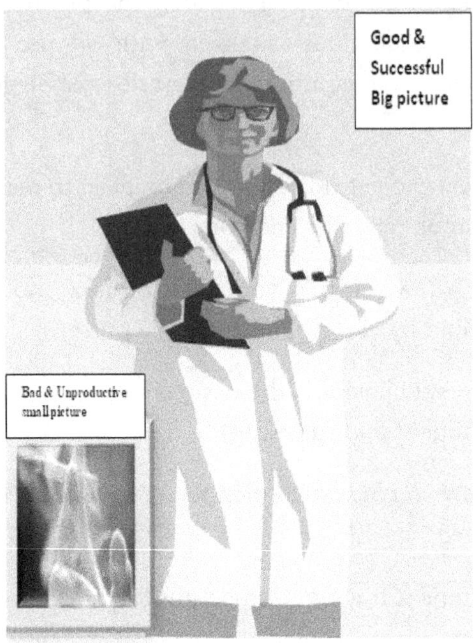

Limits of the Speaker Model

Metamodel distinctions are also known as the limits of the speaker model.

They are usually unsupported generalizations in a person's thinking. It has two components. One is a universal quantifier, and another one is the model operator.

Universal Quantifier

Universal Quantifiers in NLP are words that are universal generalizations and have no referential index. Includes words such as "all", "every", and "never". These words are very useful in formal symbolic logic, but can often be misleading out of their mathematical context

The phrase "for every x" (sometimes "for all x") is called a universal quantifier and is denoted by ∀x. The phrase "there exists an x such that" is called an existential quantifier and is denoted by ∃x.

Some examples of NLP Universal Quantifiers are as follows:

As a little side step on vocal tonality, remember that the tone up at the end of a sentence states a question, no inflection in the sentence means a statement and a downward inflection means a command. Playing around with this will help you making a shift and is useful challenging the Universal Quantifier specifically and in use of any language in general. For example, someone says to you:

"I never eat beef on Fridays."

When you want to gather more information, you might ask

"Has there ever been a time when you did?", or, "What purpose does that server?", or, "What would that lead to if you did?"

When you want to challenge their model, you can ask "Never? What would happen if you never ate it on Fridays, either?". Again, the difference here is best managed by having an open tonality in your questions. Instead of a tonality, which suggests their Universal Quantifier is a little silly or inaccurate. To challenge a universal quantifier is easy. Simply take it and turn it around as a question, either by itself, or with a question framed around it. Or, ask the person to seek out his or her own counter-example.

Words like *always, every, never, nobody, all,* and *any* are words that are used as universal quantifiers.

They are the exaggerating words, and they will exaggerate any situation.

For example, consider "I never get the right support for my work." The NLP response is, "Have you got any support at work?"

Here is another example: "Everyone dislikes me" is really "everyone dislikes you." That is the response.

Another example: "Nobody wanted to help me. The NLP response: "No one wanted to help you."

Chapter 13

Meta Model Operator of Necessity

This model indicates the lack of choices; it pushes the clients beyond the limit of acceptance. It challenges the limit by asking specific questions.

What stops you?

What could happen if you do it?

For example, "I cannot advise them anymore." The response: "What stops you?"

Another example: "I have to clean the house today." The response: "What will happen if it is not done?"

Meta Model Introduction

In today's session, we will talk about the language used in NLP. It is also called the meta model. It was discovered and developed by two psychologists, Dr. John Grinder and Dr. Bandler. So this society is very much indebted to these psychologists because they made the job easier for the coming generation to understand everyone's language and refine the output of what is helpful to both of them. It is similar to cognitive behavioral therapy (CBT) as well. If you want to outperform, if you want to have a successful life, you should mind your language.

That's why they always take your mind, determine your action, determine your fate. So we should be careful in dealing with people's language. And you can also see that successful people have a very good language that they use, a positive and upbeat language.

In this model developed by Grinder and Bandler, there are three important topics that we are going to speak about.

Before going in-depth, let us see the definition of Meta; it is the person or thing that does more than usual or that goes above and beyond. In information technology it is used as Meta tags. That's where the Meta comes in existence. In HTML they use in these programs. And sometimes, it will be visible; sometimes, it will not be visible. But they put some certain commands in it to retrieve, and they can see the tags now.

Generalizations of this kind are known in NLP as universal quantifiers and involve the use of words such as all, never, always, everyone and no-one

The three models use the specific VAKOG model that we talked about previously.

Deletion

Our minds process much information, but we recollect only the specific information that we need. For example, if you are going to the market on a specific road every day and this has been a practice for us in many occasions, sometimes we may feel that some of the shops aren't there, even though they are—our minds just didn't retain seeing them.

But when someone says there is a very good restaurant or a very good shop on the same street, our mind looks for it. And we look for it, and we see it. This is the phenomenon of deletion.

We delete information unless we are interested in getting to know some information based on our requirement. So we recollect that, and we see that picture in our mind.

Distortion

Distortion is a kind of misrepresentation that is a falsehood conceived in our minds.

Generalization

Consider the statement that all doctors are not good. We are not specific, such as stating that this one particular doctor is not helpful to us.

But in NLP, we dig in, in detail, to specify the outcome of the conversation or the language.

Another example is somebody who says that they want to own a house. And if we want to understand the conversation better, we need to ask details, all you want. You want those details to be how you're going to manage money to buy the house, how we are, how it's going to affect you. What is the result you are expecting? What are the resources you want to get?

Another example could be getting a driving license. If we need to have a basic understanding of driving a vehicle, we can achieve it by going and taking a proper driving class. We should apply for the test drive, and then we will be able to get that certification.

So NLP talks about the details that we have, and we have a conversation about how to get a specific action.

There are some questions for a category. That will help us.

One is recovering the other person's information to get into a state where the client or the other person has in mind what he wants.

To get to that certain outcome, what is the reason you want to provide a clarifying strategy or approach? All the conversations that have with one other will be on the surface level most of the time. Only with this model or people who are well versed in this can go deeper.

NLP practices will go deeper and deeper into the conversation to produce an outcome to produce good results. There are specific questions that everyone knows. For example, why weren't you out there? And these are the questions that everyone would like to have answers to. But this gives specific information about what is happening in some of the areas.

It elaborates on how we can have better results. The conversation helps in analyzing the cost of an event and why this is happening. Why do you want to do this job? The next example is how to talk about specific information: What do you want to do? What kind of house do you want it to be? The third example is, "Who is a specific question for knowing a person who did this?".

Now we go to our process of doing it—how you want to do this book, free publication, or write this essay. Or, say there's a contest at a market. So, "where is the location of the market?" is an example of the first question, then "when is the time-specific contest you are going to?" and "Get along; then, you are going to go to the market." These are the examples of what, when, where, how, and why questions.

The meta model uses the five senses for information processing; the five senses are visual, auditory, kinesthetic, olfactory, and gustatory. This produces a pattern of forms and creates the outcomes.

NLP practitioners are master practitioners; they need to understand the clients senses.

The model conceived by most of the people lacks useful information and choices; they tend to think about the conflicts and difficulties.

As per Grinder and Bandler, it is not the world that lacks choices but an individual model of the world that lacks. The universal processing model has three criteria:

1. Deletion model

2. Generalization

3. Distortion

These models help us listen to each other, communicate in a better way, and respond with the infinite answers and infinite solutions of understanding and learning from specific communication tasks.

Meta Programs

The main list of meta programs that we will concern ourselves with is as follows:

- Contemplative/Action-Oriented

- In Time (in the moment/here and now)/Through Time (sees the entire timeline)

- Independent/Team Player

- Once/Several Times

- Global (General)/Specific

- Matching/Mismatched

- Internal/External

- Toward/Away From

The most commonly used meta programs we will use are Toward/Away From and Internal/External. People who are in sales will find Matching/Mismatched and Once/Several Times applicable as well.

Contemplative/Action-Oriented

Do they take action upon receiving information or thinking about things? Are you planning to quit smoking or just thinking about it?

In Time/Through Time

People in time are in the moment, what's happening now. The future hasn't arrived; the past is gone, so the focus is on now. Over time, people visualize the entire timeline and understand what has to be done and where they are.

In-time is a common timeline type. With this time sort, a person experiences being in the present moment. Their sense of time passes through their body at some point. This timeline creates highly emotional memories and is a, therefore, a good way to remember experiences or things you want to remember.

Through Time: people will recollect their memories left to right or right to left in any other way so that all time is in front of them. To be traditionally Through Time, all of your timelines will be in front of your eyes.

Independent/Team Player

Did you move to self-employment, or can you work for someone else? Do you know people who are great to work with but never step up to leadership? Depending on the situation, some people can go both ways, depending on their comfort/skill level or if a capable leader is already in place.

Once/Several Times

Can you understand something once, or do you have to understand it several times to believe it's true? Are you getting the urge for smoking once or several times in a day?

General/Specific

Did you want to get rid of a smoking habit at once, completely, or did you want to reduce step by step, reducing the number of cigarettes that you take every day? It is the bean-counter details or the big picture. If you ask someone to describe their latest project, do they give you an overview, what they want to achieve, the goals or detail of how they are obtaining financing, or the fees they'll charge (and how it was developed)?

General-type people are bad with strategies but good in planning. Specific-type people can get details down, but they tie up loose ends.

Matching/Mismatched

Take out two different credit bills. Are there any differences you can observe? Is there someone who describes them to you or do you detailed them yourself? How do they mismatch or match? Find out more about how the bills are different or alike. Try to attempt to check out the pattern.

Internal/External

What does your internal feeling and dialogue say about quitting smoking? Do you feel positive? How do you feel if some of your friends go for a smoke? Do you feel good, or do you resist saying I am in a program to quit smoking?

How does someone feel about something great instead of going by actual facts? What do others say about internal versus external? The frame is called a reference filter.

What tells you that you must have done a great job? How did you feel good because someone said you did a good job? Or because you felt it?

Is it an external result that told you or internal outcomes?

Did you feel your sales quantity increment was successful because you saw monetary results or because you felt it?

Away From/Toward

This is the person's behavioral response of moving toward something or away from it.

If you ask a client why they want to quit smoking and they respond so they don't get cancer, they are moving away from. When they say they want to quit smoking to smell better and get healthy, they are moving toward.

Moving away is normally a response to some level of fear (moving into a community out of fear instead of the prestige of the location, for example).

People who are moving toward will explain to you the goals they need.

When you try to sell someone moving toward, and they are moving away, they'll never buy it.

Thinking can get skewed if you're dealing with a group. (For example, at training, few people make up the majority of our sessions, so it's an easy trap to fall into and not notice if someone is thinking away from or toward.)

Keep in mind that what is correct in one situation may not be good in another situation. Acceptance of uncertainty is the key symptom of mental health.

Often, the officers in charge/bureaucrats wait for their higher-ups to provide the instruction to execute actions.

That fear of making the wrong decision unintentionally becomes a system of passing the buck. Away-from thinking works like that. There is an away-from mentality in some corporate cultures, where there is a fear of taking a risk or failing. Keep in mind that the world is a complex place in which a number of decisions are made without analyzing the predictability of the outcomes.

Meta Program Exercise

Questions can also be used to talk with a client to understand their aim in a program like weight loss or smoking cessation.

1. What attempted you to attend the seminar (take an online course)?

2. What evidence did you need to know if the seminar is good?

3. What's important to you about that?

4. Do you want anything from this?

5. Did you know what that would do for you?

6. When are you going to have it?

7. What effect is it going to make in our life?

8. Will there be something that stops you from having this already?

9. Did you already have resources for this?

10. Did you need anything else?

Search for the meta programs. It's a natural skill; we're just bringing it to your conscious mind. Once you know what you're looking for, they will jump out at you.

Chapter 14

Metaphor of Change

In this section, we are going to talk about the metaphor of change. The meaning of it is the storytelling method in that we tell a story to a person, and we will convince him of the message. This is not a new technique—people used to tell stories to their kids to increase their moral value, embed commands in their mind, and have a good, socially responsible, and respectable person they involve in the story.

And from the story, they will give a moral, and they will link it to the children. Let me talk about my personal experience with the storytelling technique that I used many years ago. I got this technique from one of my NLP coaches.

A few years ago, one of my cousins, Mr. Chennai, was frustrated and disappointed with life; he had no hope for the life that he was living.

So I tried to interact with him, and I asked him many specific questions related to his family. His father was a big gambler and addicted to alcohol. And upon entering their house, they had to pass by a large wine shop.

The environment they had to pass by was really bad. It would be very difficult for somebody to manage it.

But the good part is that we keep repeating to my sister son that he should take care of his health and go to a gym to become a gym master, trainer, or coach with gym equipment.

So we built this interest in him. And he slowly started being attentive to his gym exercises. Some years later in 2011, he won third place in Mr. Chennai and second place in Mr. South India.

But we knew the environment, the genes, and the thinking requires a different approach in determining everybody's lives.

I say the genes because his father had this kind of bad behavior and bad mentality. Naturally, sometimes they say that it comes as a genetic characteristic as well.

The second one is the environment. Even if somebody wants to refrain from alcohol and all the bad habits, when entering into a house, you can see the wine shop, with all the bottles, inviting you for a drink. So we do not always have control over our environment, like we do not have control over our chromosomes. We only have control over changing our thinking; first, we embed the command; you need to build up your body so you can work hard, earn good money, and survive your life.

This embedded command helped him, and he was regularly going to the gym and participating in all the competitions and working well.

Whereas when he would come back to his house, his father would be drunk, shouting and disturbing the people who were sleeping.

So I discussed the situation with one of my coaches and he told me, let's tell him a story and just seed that good moral into his mind.

Then I found some of the good stories.

One of those stories was the monkey and the leader. Once upon a time, there was a monkey in this forest. The monkey came to some village farm and started disturbing the people around us, messing things up, throwing all the good things in with the bad. It went to the banana farm, removing the entire banana and throwing it in nearby houses there. And it spoiled the paddy field and the entire environment.

Of course, it's the character of the monkey. We cannot blame the monkey for its nature.

So the villagers thought they needed to make an effort to catch this monkey, and they wanted to return it to the forest. They then asked the village leader, and he made some arrangements with a net to trap the monkey. The monkey was jumping here and there. And they had the monkey-trapping net, and they caught the monkey and took it to the village leader. And he didn't want to put the monkey into the forest because there was something in that monkey, everybody liked it because it was so naughty, and sometimes this mysterious thing attracts people.

So the leader instead decided to find a monkey trainer. And in those days, monkey trainers trained monkeys to dance. Sometimes, they tie the monkey with rope, knots on a rope, and hold it with his hands.

So they brought the monkey, the trainer to the village leader, and the village leader said this, "Let us find one big tree without any branches, and it needs to be polished very well." Then they brought a big polished wooden pole, and they asked the monkey trainer to train the monkey to climb up and down.

The monkey trainer initially refused to take this assignment because it was a huge task to make a monkey climb on a polished structure. And the monkey cannot climb up. But somehow he trained to get it up and down, and eventually, the monkey got tired. After a few weeks and months, it became quiet. And then the trainer said, "You should go up, and the monkey followed it nicely."

So the moral of the story is our mind—we think just like this monkey, how the monkey does the thinking and dancing and all the naughty things. Of course, it is the nature of the monkey. So our mind also seems like these monkeys. It needs to be controlled. It needs to have a good output so it can be under control and help us, such as with the monkey and the people who lived near it.

I kept telling my cousin the story and told him we are like a monkey and never mind, keep wandering and everything, and keep disturbing all these rubbish things.

But if we ever focus, like the village leader and the polished wooden pole, where you want to go up and down like this monkey, it will require training and effort. So we should find the anchor. Whenever we have some disturbance in our minds, we can utilize this thinking to reduce negative thinking and benefit from our thinking process.

My cousin was soon interested in entering the gym and bodybuilding competitions, and he was finally tuned for it. And whenever he went to his house, he saw that this was an uncertain environment. It needed to be taken care of.

And when he sees his father now, he does not see him from a negative perspective and instead looks at it positively. You see, his father, because of this, alcohol, was spoiled. All his wealth, all this character is spoiled, all his work. And he did not want to fall into the same trap. Even though the opportunity was there because of the environment, he didn't want to do that.

So with these kinds of story, we can retell them to change some negative perspective to a positive perspective.

In another story, a schoolboy becomes a rich man. I told my cousin this story to help him see the importance of responsibility.

The story goes like this. A schoolboy from the village was very poor. His family could not afford a uniform for him or books and bags to carry them in. This small boy thought he needed to become a big person, a rich man. He needed to provide uniforms for poor people and provide good books for the students, and make a good studying atmosphere in the school, including clean classrooms and trees.

So he kept thinking. He worked hard. He went to many places to seek part-timework, and he did a lot of work and struggled hard to make money.

Later, he understood how to make money by creating small businesses and eventually becoming a rich man.

One day after a few years later, he came to the same school, and he told the children and teacher in front of them. He was in this school 20 years before, and his thought process was that one day he wanted to donate uniforms and books to these children and provide a better studying environment for these children here. He said, "I missed those opportunities in my good old days. I took this as a talent, not by looking at things from a negative perspective. I made a negative perspective into a positive outlook, and I achieved this after 20 years of meticulous planning and dedicated hard work and sincere thinking."

So in this story, he mentioned how we can change the negative perspective of life to a positive outlook.

I told my cousin the same thing: how you could change your mind. We are talking here about turning a negative perspective on life into a positive life perspective.

Then you eventually become a winner, perhaps a supervisor in a big private company.

So the metaphor of change is real. I gave you the practical information on how it works.

In hypnotherapy, there is also a metaphor of changing the behavior of a person. There will be some embedded comments, and those comments are purposely meant to change the behavior of the client.

So, this is all about the element of metaphor.

Chapter 15

Negative and Critical Thinking

Critical thinking is where we analyze consequences and the severity of the incidents; for example, we want to have financial independence. We want to make some investments, buy a house, own property, invest in shares, and things like that. But the point of financial independence is really about the insurance—what we need to cover us or our loved ones in case of accident or eventual death.

So this is what critical thinking discusses. Before we buy a house, we need to have some basic analysis guidelines.

- How much do we require?

- How much are we going to get a loan for?

- How many years are we going to take to repay it?

- What is the value?

- What's it going to be worth roughly after some years?

- Do you have secured insurance?

- In case of your death, how will your successors repay the money you borrowed?

- Do you have cash flow from different sources to fulfill the requirement to repay the money you have borrowed?

After this analysis, to make a decision about whether you want to take a loan or not proceed, this is what we call critical thinking. And we use it in many ways.

For example, I want to do some electrical work on the air conditioner.

- Can I accomplish this?

- What are critical factors?

- Am I trained to handle this compressor?

- Am I known to handle this electrical circuit of this air condition?

- Am I equipped to handle the proper tools required to open it to do all the repair work?

- Do I have hands-on experience in doing this repair work?

So we need to analyze these things, then we will make conclusions based on critical thinking. We can proceed with the job or not.

But in my experience, many people neglect these factors and get a hand injury and short circuits, sometimes the compressor is damaged and bursts.

So the point is that critical thinking is very important, and everyone needs to think of these critical factors before doing a small job or big task like buying a house or getting a loan from the banks.

Now I will explain what negative thinking is. Negative thinking is the thinking that will always link with the negative emotions. Let's use the same example of buying a house and getting a loan.

If you keep thinking on it negatively, you'll think thoughts like these:

- It will be a failure.

- I will not live for that much time.

- My health conditions are not good.

And if we keep giving ourselves negative feedback, you will have second thoughts not to go with the new house. Eventually, this will be programmed into your mind, which you will stop only with positive emotions. These are negative thoughts, and we need to avoid them.

Again, we can learn critical thinking, and we can analyze and adopt this thinking. But negative thing gives you a negative emotion, and that can hinder your further progress in life.

The second example, as I told for critical thinking, is air conditioning maintenance.

Many Asians don't like these air condition; people are not accustomed to the temperature and the sound it makes. Of course, now we have upgraded technology that reduces the sound like a split air conditioner. In those days, there were many box air conditioners, so these are some considerations about the air conditioning issue:

- There are many cases in which the compressors have burst.

- There are cases such as when the people sleeping inside got suffocated due to electrical short-circuiting of the air conditioning.

- Some people have been electrocuted because of the high voltages.

- Sometimes the Freon gas has escaped from the compressor, which affected the people living in the house. Some people suffocated or got lung diseases and other problems from it.

And if you don't process these with critical thinking and just keep thinking about the negative aspect of your condition, then you will not see the benefits:

- You can enjoy the climate change in the room.

- Airconditioning makes things cool and creates a comfortable condition.

- It can help you to have good sleep.

- It can be a good conditioned environment in which you can work and enjoy life.

So if you keep on thinking about these bad effects of the air conditioning, it will never end. This will be negative feedback for your mind. And eventually, on that particular equipment and its usage, you will not enjoy it, and it will tend to fail.

In summary, critical thinking is very important, and negative thoughts will always make negative feedback loops for your brain, which will stop your progress in life.

Perfectionist Thinking

We know the perfectionist will not have a good life because the perfectionist always wants to perfect things.

For example, even arranging his table, his belongings, his bedroom, his living room, or whatever it is, the perfectionist always tries to keep everything in the proper place and arrange it in a proper way.

And they think there should not be any slip-ups or inaccuracy and everything should go the way they think it should. But in life, we all have difficult roads and some failures. Life cannot go in a smooth, straight line. It will have all the pitfalls, all the ups and downs.

So you need to understand this. Sometimes, with some of my friends, if their kitchen is not arranged properly, they go mad. But we can do it by bringing housekeepers to arrange it properly if both husband and wife both are working. It will be difficult for them to keep everything in their perfect place and arrange it. Of course, telling it will be easy, but in practicality, they will have hiccups.

If you are looking for perfection in every activity that you do, it's never-ending and increases our blood pressure.

I used to think it should go like this. It did not turn out well. I started feeling too much pressure. If the job can be done by a perfectionist, it will be fine for me. Unfortunately, this did not happen.

Given the current state of the world, because everyone cannot do their job completely, we need to get help from others and learn, cooperate, and understand.

Not everyone can be a jack of all trades. The perfectionist needs to understand this to a certain degree and rethink things: "Okay, we will do critical jobs after some time. We will arrange this; we'll get help from others, and we will even learn lessons from failures; we will find some way to convert this failure into a success story." So it would be best if you could do these things. As I said, the perfectionist has a difficult time surviving in the world, especially with the current world's demands.

For example, if you are typing a letter to your president and are a perfectionist, you will look for many people's opinions in order to avoid errors. And you will get a reference even using Google? Well, it will take much time.

Instead, if you have good confidence in yourself and get minor input from here and there, you can easily complete the task. But if you are a perfectionist and you are looking for the perfect letter that you want to draft and send, it will take a lot of time, energy, and effort. So in that respect, we need to avoid being absolute perfectionists.

I'm not saying you should completely stop having a perfect outlook. It would help if you decided to a certain degree that a balanced approach in achieving the goal will be fine.

Rational Thinking

Regarding rational thinking is a very different word than how most people see it.

Rational thinking is associated with the idea that everyone needs to have a give–take situation.

Rational thinking looks for scientific facts and the evidence associated with them. And it compares what is good for all the people, or at least a majority of the people. And in this context, it doesn't neglect a small portion of people who do not know the subject.

Based on the analytical facts with the scientific evidence that we have, we can conclude that something is okay. This kind of decision will help the people in the next generation as well.

In this context, 300 years ago, if you tell a person that he can hear his family member's voice even from 3,000 kilometers away, they would have laughed at you and thought you were mentally ill.

But now, in the current reality, the moment you switch on your cell phone, laptop, or computer, the you can hear your someone's voice in a millisecond. You can send and receive live pictures and videos. It is a purely technological advancement that is helping society grow.

Now, the point here is, if we don't have rational thinking and we hide scientific facts about the transmission of the voice from one place to another place, it seems like a kind of magic. People think that there is something they can build with their stories and arguments.

But we are fortunate that the scientists put all the facts out there. How does a transmission work? The satellites from one place transfer signals with the same frequency and modulation, with all the color and brightness, in electronic form.

The receiver has the same adaptability, and they use electronic equipment to receive the signal and convert it to sound and pictures. It is so fantastic, and it's all thanks to all the scientists and innovators who brought this technology to us.

That is the essence of rational thinking: putting together the facts, analyzing them, and validating them. Sometimes scientific facts are not good for the people like Hazards in high radiations. Eventually, they upgrade, modify, and put thought and information into advanced technology, and they get a good output to protect people from this radiation sources.

Rational thinking in everyday life is essential for growth, productivity, and output.

Failure Thinking

This kind of thinking is the one that supposes that once a person has the experience of failure, he doesn't want to attempt another time.

For example, perhaps one person's marriage failed. And then he sees other married people, he gets it in his mind that he if just a failures by nature.

It's not that; there are many people who have successful married lives. And you can try a second marriage, and if that does not work, you can look for a third marriage. The world offers many opportunities, and you need to have a strong mind instead of assuming something will fail because you have the sense in your mind that you failed.

Similarly, some people say about their first job that so-and-so was hectic. And from that day onwards, they conclude they would never work under anybody. Instead, they want to have their own company. This kind of thought would never help anyone prosper in life.

We need to be careful about this failure thinking. If our first attempt fails, we can try again. If the second attempt also fails, there are many ways we can work with this, and we need to look for an alternate way of dealing with issues.

There is also a proverb: if God closes the door, He will open a window. If all doors are closed, there are still windows that we can breathe through and enjoy.

Chapter 16

Self-Talk

In this section, we will talk about self-confidence, particularly dealing with criticism in terms of the feedback that we get from the person we work for.

There is constructive criticism, and there is destructive criticism.

But even in an unhappy hour, we can approach both of these types in a very harmonious way.

For example, imagine three people:

- A is the performer. That is you.

- B is a critic.

- C is an observer.

So now be the critic. Criticize your performance or criticize your job.

In this scenario, you are dissociating oneself.

But before critically analyzing the situation, make an imaginary shield. We discussed this shield in previous chapters. You can refer to that. We need to put an imaginary shield up to protect us from these critical words, not letting them enter into your subconscious mind or your heart. So now, with shield up, look again at the situation as an observer.

In this situation as an observer, analyzes the feedback the critic made on your performance. Is it valid? Or not?

Sometimes people will say that they have the right to correct you in your job or other activity in a good way, but they don't have to abuse you.

We will keep this in mind, and you will analyze how the critic has performed his work. Dissociate yourself and observe as a third person. How can we overcome the critic's points?

Now. Shift your position from that of an observer to critic and observe, while in this position, how you handle it, seeing what your feelings are.

Then compare yourself as an observer with yourself as a critic. If you think the criticism is inappropriate, you need to see how you can handle the critique even if you feel you did not make any mistakes and the criticism was unfair.

So you can adopt a new strategy that will help you overcome the difficult situation.

But I would keep in mind that we need to reply in a professional or polished ethical way so as not to spoil your career and relationship with the other person.

So this needs to be kept in mind. And if you keep practicing it for some time, you can analyze where you are, your work, or your activities in some other place.

Self-Appreciation

Self-appreciation is self-taught. You can motivate yourself by appreciating yourself. Just now, we talked about three people:

- Performer

- Observer

- Appreciator instead of critique.

We need to make people who appreciate that are an appreciator or the appraiser. So you need to see the submodality and see the reaction of how you feel comfortable and confident you are when somebody appreciates the activity you perform.

Now, be the observer and see the reaction of the performer, how you react to this appreciation. If it is helpful, it will help you experience other similar scenarios.

The same kind of happiness we have when we are facing some appreciation has now shifted to the theater. You put yourself in that place and start appraising the performer. You will see the reaction and see what words trigger a happy moment and how this kind of simple work helps motivate you to use your potential, get more output, and get more performance out of it.

There is also technique you can use to increase self-esteem. You need to look into the mirror that you see every day. When you wake up, in front of the mirror, tell yourself you love yourself. This is a basic thing that you can do to increase your self-appreciation. Tell the mirror things like these:

- I love you.

- I thank you.

- I forgive you.

- I'm sorry.

If you keep telling the mirror these things, it indirectly helps you increase your self-motivation and self-esteem. So if you continue this practice, it will help you be a better person with motivation after some time.

Semantically Ill-Formed

Semantic information is based on improper responsibility or assumption or judgment; it is a kind of distortion. It is an unsubstantiated belief rather than one based on facts.

There are three subtitles:

- Cause and effect, also known as perceived responsibility

- Mind reading, based on assumption

- Low performance, based on judgment

Cause and Effect

The cause is an action and the effect is the result.

So how does A cost the arm of B?

It is the connection between the action and the after-effect, which is the result of the action.

For example, "Your report makes me unhappy." The response is how your report makes a person unhappy.

In another example, "I am angry that you never keep your promises." The response is how my lack of fulfillment of promises makes you angry.

Mind Reading

Based on an assumption, not on fact, the speaker believes that another person's feedback is not actual.

How good is the term "mind-reading" in this case?

Mind reading also involves the feeling, thinking, and meaning of others, how they feel and interact.

For example, "Most people think he's bad." The response is, "How, specifically, is he bad?"

Another example: "I'm not too fond of parties." The response: What specifically don't you like about parties.

Or, "I never want to go to work." The response is, "Why specifically don't you want to go to work?"

Low Performance

This is based on judgment, and it's a kind of generalization.

The speaker uses this model: "of/for whom?"

For example: "This is not going to work out. The response: "This is not going to work out for whom?"

Another example: "It's failed." The response: "This failed for whom?"

Chapter 17

Escape Formula for Loneliness

This is an important formula for loneliness. In the current micro-level families, we see people with only one child and maybe two children. Also we see both parents working. They find little time to spend with the children. In this scenario, the children suffer loneliness.

When they grow up, they want to be isolated, and they want to be raised. They want to have the work-alone attitude. There is no teamwork with them. So their focus will be only on themselves, not other people, not society. There are advantages and disadvantages to this approach.

My friend, a resident of a developed country, came to Saudi Arabia for a project, and I had a very good interaction with him. He mentioned that in schools they always talk about the following:

- You should always be productive.

- You should always think about innovation.

- You should always be discovering new things

- You should put more effort into building the nation.

- You should invent new things with science adventures.

What had been taught in the school?

What does happen to these continuous embodied thoughts?

It helps them become successful scientists and discoverers, but they desperately lack a social life and family life. Maybe five to ten years ago, the government changed its approach to us, society, and especially the family. Now it recognizes the value of the family, and it has started giving children more if they can build a family based on goodness, fix up their family ethics and values, and respect and take care of their parents, especially when they are aged and living alone.

One hundred years before, this situation was different, and the government paid more attention to innovation and discovery. Right now, you see that it is thinking more about family values and helping good parents, not leaving them alone in an isolated place. (These are all things I heard from my friend.)

People start realizing human value when they get older. We should have some system to take care of them. I'm not saying there should be old age homes everywhere and that they should put their parents in that home. If two children are studying abroad or working abroad, then there would be a big vacuum in the family, especially for the parents.

The mother or the father might pass away. The surviving parent will face loneliness, a different kind of loneliness because they will be alone under these circumstances. There are some tips I want to provide you that will help you overcome the loneliness.

1. We should have a time chart of the activities that we will do this week and next week. And you can make it as much as you can do for a maximum of one month. After this scheduling, every activity will be accountable. We need to have some gaps to bridge in case some emergency activities appear that need our attention more. So if you make the schedule, it will occupy your mind, and it will correctly guide you in a structured way to do the activities. It will

also help you get rid of unnecessary thoughts that can come to the surface of your mind.

2. Plan for a physical activity. Some people like swimming, or perhaps playing tennis, brisk walking, or going to the gym. That will be great, and that will help exhaust you and add energy to your system. The fresh air helps the circulation of the blood. You will be free in the fresh air, and you will feel that you are in an energized state.

3. We need to have a proper dieting plan, and we should have a focus on food habits. Junk food causes too much craving of high-calorie food in the long run and does not help us in building muscles or a strong physique. It will just cause you to accumulate cholesterol, and you'll just gain additional weight. So we need to focus on our food habits.

4. You should also plan time for hobbies. Perhaps writing a poem. Some people tend to read a lot of non-technical fiction stories. So we need to focus on these extracurricular activities like reading, writing, and watching TV, which gives you relaxation. But you need to do it in segments. For example, Monday, I want to speak to my friend, and say I'll be off writing an essay on this topic. On Wednesday, I want to watch my favorite TV show. Thursday, I want to spend half an hour reading some specific articles from this website. So we need to make these arrangements. Of course, I will provide a template of how we are going to have this. And if we find some relaxation time, for example, on off days like Friday or Saturday, we are going to utilize these days in useful, productive ways like engaging in social activity, social media, or some online courses. Or you can also watch some online lectures. So these are some options. If you explore them one by one based on your interest, you can focus on.

5. We need to cultivate good sleeping habits. We should confine our thoughts. Then you go to bed.

    a. We should say to ourselves, "Whatever happened to the world or whatever happened to us. Let us sleep."

    b. Let Almighty take care of it, and relax. And you need to sleep in a very peaceful way.

    c. Let whatever is happening tomorrow rest. Your meeting with the GM or the president, whatever it is, when you enter your bed, you need to tell your mind you are just going to sleep. Forget about whatever is happening to you and whatever is happening around the world. It doesn't matter to you right now. And you want to relax 100 percent and have a good, relaxed sleep

    d. Some programs can help you get to a very deep, transcendental state of sleep that will start in your dreams. In the morning when you wake up, you will be full of natural energy. One technique is from NLP. The other is hypnotherapy. And if you don't want to engage in all these things, you can go to a gym. And some gym masters can teach techniques for relaxation. And I do have a solid sleep. And similarly from yoga classes also. There are some techniques they will give us to make you fall into a good and deep sleep. There are also YouTube videos that can be helpful for people who may not be able to get out to these places, etc.

6. Don't have monotonous activities in your schedule. You need to have different tasks every week, say, learning a new language, or watching a new program. That kind of thing will help you to get motivated in other fields. Also, supposing you are interested in only mathematics, perhaps

divert your attention to some language skills. Then you see the difference, though you may not have interest in it. You will see additional knowledge that you gain from it over time. And perhaps you can concentrate on some financial sectors out there in the market—selling and buying shares, that kind of thing—which will not only help you in knowledge but may also help you financially.

7. Consider volunteering yourself: Engaging in community service lets you interact with the community. There may be a forum like the Toastmasters club or some club wherein you can associate with others. You can meet different kinds of people and interact with them. You give your speech, thoughts, ideas, and you can also learn the thoughts and opinions of others, which will enrich your life.

8. You should also have a self-improvement agenda. Make part of your work a self-improvement agenda. For example, say you want to read one self-improvement book. If that book contains a page of 300 pages, say you read five pages every day. But you need to make it a small segment. So you start focusing on this self-improvement book. There are many tips that the author will provide in every book. There is an important subject that will be there, like cream, and if you taste it, it will add flavor to your life. So, in that respect, you have a constant focus in developing yourself. You can also join as some kind of online course that will help you with your self-study.

9. Motivation triggers vital potential. Some people, if they interact with the friends and relatives, have enormous joy and enormous happiness. So you are adopting a strategy that motivates you, You will get more focused energy. Maybe once a week or twice a week.—that will help you to get on the right track.

10. Plan every week to do some window shopping, and every week change the location to another place. There is a lot of window shopping available. It's not necessary to go in and buy things. But you can go, and you can visit a lot of multistory shopping malls, and you can see different kinds of people and different materials and different things from around the world. There are a lot of electronic items, books, and perfumes. There are many food items also. So you don't need to buy everything, but you can just relax and see them. There are also various shops, like the fancy store for watches; there are hundreds of kinds of watches displayed there, from very costly diamond watches to normal watches. And there are vitamin shops that you can walk to, and you can see the different new products that will help with your muscle. I hope these tips will help you in overcoming loneliness.

Chapter 18

Strategies

Adopt an analytical strategy, which is a structured approach to a complicated problem, a complex situation that we're in, such as family-related issues. And you want to do a proper analysis with these strategies.

A strategy is a structured and skillful way to analyze all sorts of things, from financial issues to emotional issues. Then we will know the pluses and minuses of say, keeping a relationship or not; sometimes, there is some physical ailment, and we need to consider the hormonal imbalances that also constitute this kind of difference of opinion or difficult situation. Perhaps that person is less physically unable to cope and does not have the same adaptability we do.

Physical compatibility strategy

Physical compatibility is the ability of husband and wife to be used together without ill effect, based on the physical domains and how they understand in their character, values, and beliefs. It can also be understood as of physical intimacy, an act or reaction, such as expressing feelings including close friendship, platonic love, romantic love, or sexual attraction. Examples of physical intimacy include being inside someone's personal space, holding hands, hugging, kissing, caressing, and sexual activity.

If you feel as though you and your partner are sexually incompatible, there are some things you can do. Consider seeing a therapist or, specifically, a sex therapist, to determine the underlying reasons you and your partner aren't enjoying sex together.

To know if you are compatible with someone, you trust them. You know they are and always will be honest with you, you don't question their love or doubt their level of commitment to the relationship, you can be at your most vulnerable and exposed moment and know, without a doubt, that they won't leave, that they'll stay even when things get ugly and rough, that.

How do people cooperate in response to the questions on physical attributes, including all the physical efforts, meaning making their partners happy and healthier and leading to the next step? So, in the physical aspects of this, the compatibility should be good enough. I mean, the physical force and the energy of both partners should be at a congruent point that they both meet their needs.

Mental Strategy

The mental strategy is the mental process that each one can build in issues on the male/female sides from their parents, relatives, or society.

How are they going to cope with issues in individual mental stability?

If they are not mentally stable, they will play a blame game. So we need to understand mental stability and capability.

How are they playing the blame game? If this blame game is biased, then needs to be reconsidered to be given enough information, enough evidence about it. And we need to talk about it.

Why does the blame game happen? It is purely the inability of one person to accomplish a task, so they just blame the other person.

Financial Strategy

Sometimes a financial strategy is important because men want to make money, work hard, and come home with the money and run the family.

Supposing somebody wants to take a loan to buy a house. If they make this a strategy, they need to continue working on the other side. But perhaps the partner doesn't want to have this house. They would prefer to roam around and spend money, living happily like this.

Then this draws completely parallel lines. These lines do not cross. Of course, there are always exceptions in life, but we are not talking about those—we're talking about the lessons learned from these issues, especially those I have undergone. I want to pass this lesson to the people who read this book to benefit them, at least at some point in time.

We talk about financial stability so one can think of becoming financially independent.

That person can think that he can still see ways how his family members repay him in his absence.

They may have skills and knowledge that will help them have a good friend circle, and they may have relatives' support to have a good alternative so that they can manage the repayment.

And if they are positive-minded, they will get confidence in this aspect; the family will survive more tough issues.

Social Adaptability Strategy

Social Adaptability is the ability to form and maintain friendships according to one's peer group's norms. The level of social competence of any person. It's an adjustment and adaptation to humans to other individuals and community groups working together for a common purpose.

Social adaptability is certainly something; in social adaptability we will be lagging. It's not our issue because, in developed countries, they parties for kids and things like that to nurture them. So in the absence of this strategy, we will have a difference of opinion. Ways to enhance our Adaptability Skills

- Change Your Thought Process. Let go and take it easy principle of the "Well, that's the way we've always done it" mentality.

- Force Yourself to Take Risks. Little progress is made without risk.

- Encourage Others to Be Open-Minded. open mind is to accept others point of view as well.

If no older people are involved in passing on what is right or wrong, who can view the opinion of both the husband and wife or both of them, giving suggestions and providing justice? The older people restrain us from avoiding unnecessary thinking. In the absence of that social strategy, we will have many unsolved problems.

So one has to be able to employ these four strategies.

If you want to have a good, happier life, use amicable strategies to have a peaceful life.

Chapter 19

Negative to Positive Life Experiences

In life, there are negative and positive circumstances. Does that make us feel nervous?

There are many such examples of negative circumstances that have happened in my life. I have at least a few points I would like to add here.

One example is that my travel to Saudi Arabia for employment for this new company was an afternoon flight. I prepared myself with two suitcases full of new clothes and some edible items that my wife put in and under that briefcase.

But I wasn't looking forward to this new job, though it would give me a wonderful experience abroad and monetary benefits. Furthermore, changing to a petrochemical company from oil and gas industry I was in meant I would lose credibility for future experience in oil/gas. My ultimate aim was to have a family together with my wife; and with that came thoughts of working abroad. I sacrificed my professional growth, and my main focus was just to go ahead and enjoy family life.

But before coming to the airport, I got a phone call from my wife's friend. We had been discussing the working environment and the circumstances that we come across in Gulf countries, how one can look and handle all those things. And they pointed out that there would be some loneliness, and there should be some sacrifice. We need to adapt and accept those realities of life. So with that precaution, I became determined to have a family life and get out.

It was a five-and-a-half hour journey from my place to fly to Dubai, and from Dubai I had to travel to Dammam. It was an evening flight. I had to report three hours early to the airport. So I prepared myself at 10 a.m. with my suitcase ready.

My mother in law and their family called me and some personally came, and they booked a taxi, and I took the taxi from my place to the airport, which was approximately 20 km away.

With many different scenarios going on my mind and exploring the possibility of a good life, I'm just moving toward the airport. On the way, there was a very big pothole in the road. The driver did not notice it, and the vehicle just jumped into it. Suddenly it stopped. I took a deep breath; then, I saw that the tire was almost 60 percent in the pothole. Then I thought, is this a negative sign? Negative circumstance? Then I reconciled myself—I didn't know. I thought things like, "Now, let's not think this is superstitious thinking. Let's move forward because you have plenty of time. Let's not make a big deal." The driver asked me to get out, so I did, and I put some stones and wooden planks under the tire he got from his car, and he put it there and the tire jumped and rolled over and out of the pothole. I was watching this scenario, and unconsciously it created negative thinking.

Positive thinking can help you control anxiety on the other hand Negative thoughts can increase your worry or fear. NLP can help you replace negative thoughts with accurate, encouraging ones. Changing your thinking will take some time.

A common stress, sleep disturbance, can leads to negative thoughts. In most of the cases, depression can be caused by negative thinking.

But my coaches always said if you come across a circumstances like this, just make a shield. Positive energy flows across your body, and that positive energy will help you achieve greatness and positivity. I did that, and the car moved smoothly. There are two terminals in the airport, and I did not notice the two terminals, though I used to travel to the same airport frequently, but that time there was also no separation.

I approached security for entry purposes. Then I realized I had to go to the international flight section.

I was completely absent-minded, and I was thinking and moving in my mind screen, picturing everything that happened from that first interview up to the time I was getting onto the flight, and some negative thoughts came with me, like the blood samples and physically checking for sicknessfor the employment medical test at the company.

Those kinds of things came to my mind, and they disturbed me. I did not resign from my company, though I wrote a resignation letter, and I told my wife to hold onto it. If I felt okay, then she could send that letter. But many of my friends knew, and I told them that I was looking for another opportunity.

We have one month's notice period to get relieved from the present employer. It wasn't a big deal because I still had rotational off days only. So all these scenarios and many other thoughts keep coming to my mind and bothering me, and I didn't have a concentrated focus.

I consoled my mind and walked. After all the formalities were completed, the check-in procedure was completed. Then, I was restless from the thinking that came to my mind the night before. I did not sleep well because it was a big move, and many decisions and disturbances were going on in my mind. So I entered into the airplane and got seated, and it was going fine, and then, within a half hour of landing, there was heavy turbulence on the aircraft.

My heart started palpitating. There were strange things happening around me and in me.

The turbulence was so heavy, and I could see that there was a real problem in the aircraft. As I mentioned, because I am a frequent flyer, I know the disturbance that can happen due to the weather. Then I prayed to God to rescue me because that kind of turbulence can cause a crash.

The pilot, who had high technical confidence, managed to make a safe crash landing. But he did it in a very professional way that did not affect any of us. In that process, there was a delay of half an hour, and after getting out of the aircraft, the check-in procedure delayed us for another one and a half hours. So we lost two hours in this process. The air turbulence made turbulence in my own thinking about whether I needed this job. Then I put those thoughts aside. I went to the Dubai airport, and the flight to Dubai to Saudi Arabia was canceled, another hiccup.

The travel agents arranged a temporary hotel stay, and they gave me food and accommodation slips. The next flight would be in two days. So, in those two days in Dubai, many thoughts came to my mind, and I was upset.

With the training my coaches provided, I could overcome this trauma. I told myself that it's all part of life, and I needed to move to the next level.

There were many passengers to Dammam that I interacted with. They had been talking about going around Dubai and visiting the malls. But I did not explore Dubai. I just wanted to stay in the hotel. I walked around the lobby and saw the different flowers and fountains, experiencing the architectural amazement in the Hilton hotel lobby.

After two days, the flight was ready. I landed safely this time in Dammam, my first check-in in Saudi Arabia.

So far, after a midnight check-in and taking all the files and reviewing the associated documents, it took a long time. It was around 2.00 a.m. in the airport. One of our Indian drivers was receiving me. There was a communication delay. I was informing the company, as well as my wife.

And when I spoke to my wife, I tried to sound confident so she wouldn't know that internally I had had negative impact. I was having thoughts of returning to my hometown. But it went well.

The Indian driver received me at the airport, and the climate was very hard, with 100% humidity, sometimes more than 38°C at night. And I could see the hot waves coming across the sand and hitting our skin. While driving to the hotel, we had a discussion, and he explained his experience with the Gulf countries.

He talked about two things: you need to have patience when working abroad and never really lose your temper. That is the only advice he gave me. Also he explained that his life was destroyed. When he was working in a small company as a technician, he had a fit of anger in an argument with his boss. His inability to do multiple tasks had driven his anger, and that anger caused him to be lowered from the technician job to driver. He was very kind and again reiterated that one needs to have much patience when working in Gulf countries. I listened to him patiently, receiving the advice and his elaborate instructions for working in Gulf countries.

And I took to heart the positive note that I should have patience. Then he dropped me at the hotel, and he also got me a calling card so I could call home. That calling card was very useful for some days until I got a new phone connection.

We reached a Jubail destination and the hotel accommodation. In that hotel, I took a bath and relaxed for some time. After this tiresome journey, I felt drowsy and decided to go bed so I could get up early in the morning. Suddenly, at 5 a.m., the cot fell down, though I was not injured. I remained worried for a little while but realized it's a very strange, bad experience that was happening to me.

I was seized by a sense of bad omens: crash landing, and then the broken cot. All this nonsense. Then I managed to move, changed my clothing, and went to the front desk. I told them about the cot issues. And then they changed the cot within an hour.

Then, that night, I had disturbed sleep.

And the scenarios were running in my mind.

So the next day, exactly at 7:00, the same driver picked me up from the hotel. He advised me, "Sir, never forget the advice they give you. Don't lose your temper. We need to have tons of patience to work in Gulf countries."

Then, with that note, I entered the car. He took me to a small Indian restaurant on the way to the new company. It was a Farman restaurant opposite the Riyadh Bank. The proprietor, a gracious Kerala man, was a friend of our driver and greeted us. "Assalam Alaikum! Welcome to Saudi Arabia. Insha Allah, you will have wonderful days here. We have traditional food here. Enjoy the taste."

"Alaikumassalam. Thanks," I said.

I saw a heap of bondas, vadai, stacked thin chapattis and parottas, boiled eggs in one rack and on the other rack chocolate muffins and some vanilla cakes. I could smell boiling tea and roasting dasos on the hot pan. One can understand the smells, decoration, and cleanliness without even tasting the stuff. I reacted, salivating. And we queued up for our traditional food.

The driver also showed me the places where I could get Indian stuff, the grocery store, and other places. I was very fascinated with him. He was a very grateful guy, and I'm thankful to him for the pieces of advice and the encouragement he gave to me to have many years of continued service in that company.

We reached the security booth, and the company's security askedme, "Will you provide your passport?"

I didn't answer the question. He reiterated again, 'Would you like to go inside the company and hand me your passport?'

"No, in my experience with my previous company, no one takes my passport. If possible, every day, as long as I enter the company, I will provide a copy, not the original."

"Oh, no. Impossible. You can't do that. They will surely take the real passport only, not a scan. We will not allow you inside."

What I learned later in conversations with friends was that security requirements are very different.

I was so annoyed that the staff that I wasn't allowed to enter unless I gave them my passport. And he was talking to me in his language, which I could not understand.

I was so annoyed but tried to cover it up by asking the security the next question: "Can I provide a scanned copy of the passport?"

The driver came to the rescue and said this was the procedure, and I had to give them the passport, and when I was going home, security would return it. It would be this waytillIgot a resident permit.

I said, "My apologies, I could not understand the system and this passport requirement. Suppose if by mistake, anything happened to my passport—it's an invitation to lots of trouble."

Then we went to the administrative office. The driver introduced us, and I was happy to speak to them. Then we went over into media, perhaps around 9 a.m., and they said they had been looking forward to my arrival.

We met many people, and it was fantastic entrance.

But suddenly I heard a fire alarm at 10:00 a.m. And people were moving here and there, and I learned about the company's emergency assembly point. You need to assemble there, and they will call for attendance. Then we need to go one by one, announcing our presence. And if your friends are not there for any other reason, we need to provide justification. All the formality will takes a lot of time.

In the meantime, I saw huge black fumes coming.

Luckily, nothing happened to anyone in the office. A fire engine came, and they put out the fire. The fire was due to some electrical charge circulating on the AC compressor, and it was a hot summer day.

So, again, there was more negative thinking, another bad omen for my thinking pattern. And I was again not feeling happy.

At the end of the day, I returned to my hotel room feeling sad. I had the same driver, who had this encouraging word: "Sir, forget about it. These things will happen in life. Just proceed. You will achieve success. You will get the victory." And in the evening, the driver came to my room, maybe around 7:00. And we started discussing this, and he mentioned that if you have this difficulty, there is one rescue method that will make negative thinking go away from you. The bad thing around you will go away.

I did tell all my stories to the driver and the driver said, "Just pray to God. When you have a residence permit, you will be allowed to travel, and you can have peace of mind."

You visit the Holy cities, and then I'm sure you will feel happiness. Then in the meantime, after 8:00, they called from my company in

India, asking my location and what I was doing, all those things. Then I explained that I was still in my off days.

I told them, "I'm looking for another opportunity. I will surely let you know. But give some time for me to think and make that reply." They send official mail to me saying, "We need to know, are you coming back to the job?"

You want to go from you want to take another sentiment, new opportunity that you are already looking for. Then, again, the driver told me, whatever happened. It's gone for good. But don't ponder around, thinking and thinking. Well, we're thinking, and that will destroy your happiness. You have made some decision to come here, and let us stick with that thinking."

After two days, I called my wife and told her the resignation letter was an email in my inbox as a draft. I told her, "You can send it. I'm okay with this."

In the meantime, my company in India asked my wife many, many times, about my whereabouts and job. And in that process, my wife also got upset because she had two small kids to take care, and people kept asking this unnecessary question.

Naturally, things get tensed. And my wife was always a straightforward woman. And she was never afraid about speaking out or hiding the truth. For some reason, she never does that. She always speaks the truth, and what comes to mind? She will talk irrespective of my being her husband or any other thing. So in that way, we find it very difficult, and she told me all that happened.

Then I also told to my company in India about my resignation. I mentioned I was looking for another opportunity. And I thanked them for management's support during the seven years of my tenure. I was indebted to them. All those things were in my resignation letter. And the process was complete.

The point here is I went from a comfort zone to an unknown zone because I didn't have any relatives. I didn't know anybody in this new location.

The new area was tough, but I got through it.

There are a lot of bad omens, bad symptoms. So you can take it with superstition, or you can take it differently.

But if you want to add to this success, you need to bear the pain that comes with it. There is no cakewalk for the next opportunity that we will take, and that opportunity may be very fruitful and enjoyable.

With that note, I concluded that life always gives you opportunity, and you need to adapt, accept, and look for the changes from the uncomfortable zone to the comfort zone, from the comfort zone back to the uncomfortable zone. But life always gives us the opportunity to prosper and grow.

Chapter 20

NLP Practitioner Practical Treatments Questions and Answers

a) **How would we use NLP to treat an addiction to these habits of smoking, alcohol, sex, or food?**

I prefer to use the Swish Pattern technique. I will ask the patient to get the behavior of these bad habits in a visual picture in mind, using all the visual, auditory, and kinesthetic elements in this picture.

Now imagine a big powerful picture with higher length and width in nature.

I will ask him to diminish or shrink the bad picture into a dot inside the good big picture.

Project the good big picture into a bigger size with all brightness and all color and contrast.

Do this process mentally, five to ten times rapidly.

After several times, test the patient—the old behavior picture won't be the same as before.

b) **How would we use NLP to increase sports performance?**

I will ask the client to do the Circle of Excellence technique.

I will ask him to imagine a stage or a circle when he was victorious, comfortable, confident, successful, with all the submodalities associated with it. When he has formed the mental pictures two or three times, I ask him to have a figure anchor touching his right-hand thumb and forefinger and say "power" or "excellent" in his mind or verbally.

Now move on to the future sporting image of an excellent performance and enter the same circle of excellence; imagine the circle has many blessing and ask him to use the anchor again.

Now I will ask him to leave the circle and think about what he can do differently in the future to achieve this success.

c) How would we use NLP to overcome family miscommunication issues?

The meta model is simply a set of tools that establishes better communication, which helps your client communicate more clearly.

Ask what, how, and who in response to the specific form of the client's language.

Your skills as a meta modeler depend on your willingness and ability to implement the questions and the responses provided by the meta model.

d) How would we use NLP to overcome public speaking issues like fear of being in front of people, lack of confidence due to speaking with an accent?

I use the movie theater model for overcoming fear, using booth, movie, and chair.

I would ask the client to sit in the booth operator area and ask him to review a bad experience as though he is watching the movie, with all black-and-white visual submodalities, slowly.

Then I will ask him to imagine the same situation differently as though he were on the screen.

Third, I will ask him to move to watch it again from the audience seats. On that frozen frame, you leave the projection booth and slip back into the present you, down there in the middle of the theatre.

Step into the freeze-frame of the younger you, who feel okay again, as the movie, come to an end. It is a double dissociation.

Then I will ask him to run the same scene backward and in color as fast as he can.

I will use resource anger for his safety on his shoulder. It is for safety in feeling good. Test the process—attempt to return to the phobic state however you can.

What if you were in that situation at present? When would you expect the same situation next?

If you still get a phobic response, you need to repeat Steps 1 to 4 exactly, but faster each time, until none of the phobic response remains.

e)   How would we use NLP to overcome street anger?

I would recommend using chaining anchors and elicit dissociation.

"Look at yourself from my point of view."

"Pretend you're in a movie theater, watching yourself on the screen."

Anchor this dissociated state: Anchor #1:Elicit Stuck (Problem) State

Anchor: Anchor #2: Chain to Dissociation

Fire Anchor #2, which is Stuck/Problem, and fire Anchor #1 with you on the screen.

Test—Have your client think of stuck/problem.

f)   How would we use NLP to have weight loss programming?

I will use the Future Pace technique.

Rehearse mentally and physically so a specific behavior will occur naturally in a certain situation.

An extremely useful tool is to "future pace" yourself into already thinking of having completed the weight loss.

What will you feel, hear, and see at that moment in time?

You experience this looking through your eyes.

If you are going to seek inspiration for weight loss, pick a true model of excellence!

It is best to find someone who claims to be an expert in personality development or coaching tools that has done it or looks the part.

How will you feel confident and successful that completing your weight loss goal will affect your life?

How will it affect others around you?

Describe the details of your values.

What are the advantages of having a healthy body as part of a healthy life, which is true to your values?

Using NLP will help with weight loss.

Understand the negative intention behind overeating.

What are the positive things that are going to be brought out by these changes?

Will you have comfort? Enjoyment?

What are alternative ways for you to achieve this rather than avoiding overeating?

What are anchors in your circumstances that cause you to overeat?

What are the hurdles that stop you from achieving your goals?

g) How does the swish exercise help someone?

The Kinesthetic Swish Exercise can help a person in rough times or in social situations.

Using NLP techniques, we can help a person in need.

Recognize and anchor yourself where the person is with a light touch on the shoulder, wrist, or hand.

Ask them to focus their attention on your hand and point it downward.

Keep the pacing state.

Mention phrases such as, "Things will be fine," "Look up with confidence," and "Brighten up in the future" as you pull your hand upward.

As you move your hand up, and preferably to the person's right side, release the anchor.

If possible, repeat the technique.

Calibrated loop:

It is an ongoing interaction between two or more people in which specific behaviors of each person trigger specific responses in each other.

h) Describe metamodel in few sentences?

A model of language focuses on words people use to delete, distort, generalize, limit, or specify their realities.

It provides a series of outcome-specific questions used to recover lost information and/or loosen rigid patterns of thinking.

Lead system: The representational system of a person that will be used to access stored information.

i)   Describe strategies in few sentences?

The internal thinking process a person uses to make a decision is a strategy.

For example, when you were ordering food, what was your approach/process?

You follow a particular process, whether you realize it or not. It may be auditory or visual.

Then you make your decision, close the menu, and make your order.

These motivational meta programs influence a person's communication/perceptual style. Each person has some auditory, kinesthetic, visual, and digital combination, with one of these acting as a predominant style. The meta programs also affect a person's behavioral style. There will be a combination of expressive, dominant, steady, or analytical, with one or two predominant styles.

A person must communicate using his primary communication/ perceptual style or model.

You must also understand the behavior style and the actions that are presented in response to that.

Chapter 21

Further NLP Understanding References

Adler, H. (1994). *NLP: The new art and science of getting what you want*, Piatkus Books.

Andreas, S., & Andreas, C. (1988). *Change your mind and keep the change*, Real People Press.

Andreas, S., & Andreas, C. (1989). *Heart of the mind: Engaging your inner power to change with neuro-linguistic programming*, Real People Press.

Andreas, S., & Andreas, C. (1966). *Core transformation*, Real People Press.

Andreas, S., & Faulkner, C. (1966). *NLP: The technology of achievement*, Nicholas Brealey Publishing Ltd.

Bandler, B. (1985). *Using your brain for a change*, Real People Press.

Bandler, R., & Grinder, J. (1989). *The structure of magic: A book about language and therapy* (vol. I), Science and Behavior Books.

Bandler, R., & MacDonald, W. (1988). *An insider's guide to submodalities*. Meta Publications: Cupertino, CA.

Brooks, M. (1990). *Instant rapport*, Time Warner International.

Cameron-Bandler, L. (1978). *They lived happily ever after*, Meta Publications.

Cameron-Bandler, L., Gordon, D., & Lebeau, M. (1985). *Know how*, Meta Publications.

Cameron-Bandler, L., Gordon, D., & Lebeau, M. (1985). *The emprint method*, Meta Publications.

Colloca, L. (2018). *Neurobiology of the placebo effect* (Part I), Cambridge: MA, United States.

Colloca, L. (2018). *Neurobiology of the placebo effect* (Part II; 1st ed.), Cambridge: MA, United States.

Dilts, R. (1990). *Changing belief systems with NLP*, Meta Publications.

Dilts, R. (1996). *Visionary leadership skills*, Meta Publications.

Dilts, R., Hallborn, T., & Smith, S. (1990). *Beliefs*, Metamorphous Press.

Dilts, R., & Cameron-Bandler, L. (1980). *Neuro-linguistic programming*, Meta Publications.

Farrelly, F., & Bandsman, J. (1978). *Provocative therapy*, Meta Publications.

Gordon, D. (1989). *Therapeutic metaphors: Helping others through the looking glass*, Gordon Meta Publications.

Richardson, J. (1987). *The magic of rapport*, Meta Publications

Shapiro, A. K., & Shapiro, E. (2006). *The powerful placebo: From ancient priest to modern physician*, JHU Press.

Pease, A., & Pease, B. (2004). *The definitive book of body language*, Random House.

Glossary of Common NLP Terms

Accessing cues – Behaviors of a person, including eye movements, postures, and breathing.

Anchor – Astimulus using our senses to produce results.

Auditory – Having to do with the sense of hearing.

Break state – Changing the mental state and focus.

Behavioral flexibility – Modifying the behavior of a person, adapting changes in a person's behavior.

Calibrate – To observe another person's nonverbal behavior.

Chaining anchors – A series of anchors set up to produce specific positive results.

Chunking – Making bigger tasks into smaller tasks.

Collapsing Anchors – Firing several anchors simultaneously to produce a new outcome.

Congruent – Aligning your outcomes with your beliefs or values.

Dissociated – State of experiencing from the outside rather than analyzing internally.

Distortion – Response of a person changed for some reason. It is an internal representation distorted in some ways.

Environment – The effects on the whole system of a person of the neighboring people and surroundings.

Embedded command – Set of statements intended to produce desired results.

Eye accessing cues – Changes in the eye movements.

Flexibility – The state of having many choices.

Future Pace – Mentally rehearsing a behavior for you currently, hoping to produce a specific future result.

Gustatory – Sense of taste.

Incongruent – Misalignment of thoughts and outcomes.

Intension – The purpose of your behavior.

Kinesthetic – Sense of feeling.

Lead system – The approach or pattern you use to access your internal pieces of information.

Leading – Helping someone move in a certain direction.

Lost performative – Pattern in which the person was acting to provide opinion, without having the facts. In other words it is any judgement or opinion. When the source of the judgement or opinion is not available. So often taken decision based on the beliefs and opinions

Map of reality – A person's perception of reality.

Metamodel – A set of questions and answers designed to overcome deletion, distortion, generalization, limitation, or specification of realities.

Metaphor – A storytelling technique, that is relevant and symbolic, which allows us to bypass conscious mind resistance of the client and to have the client make connections at a deeper inner level.

Meta-outcome – The desired outcome that is more general than the stated one.

Milton model – Language patterns useful for delivering a message by hypnotherapist Milton.

Mirroring – Matching a behavior with another person.

Modal operators – A specific set of language patterns to do evaluations of action.

Modality – One of the five senses.

Modeling – Analyzing and adopting proven successful process structures to replicate to others.

Negative results – A failure or resourceful outcome that is stated in the negative.

Nest – To fit one thing within another thing.

Nominalization – Language pattern for words that has no physical existence as things. Examples of nominalizations are "love", "freedom", "happiness", "respect", etc.

Olfactory – Sense of smell.

Outcome – Desired or produced result.

Pacing – Copying and repeating another person's behavior.

Perception filter – A perspective about an object, a person, and situations.

Polarity response – A reverse response from the previous position.

Predicates – A word expressing a person's representational system.

Preferred representational system A person's preferred use of the representational system.

Presupposition – Core belief in NLP.

Rapport – Trust and relationship established between people.

Reframing – Making difference frame to an experience

Representational systems – The five senses of the human being:visual, auditory, kinesthetic, gustatory, and olfactory.

Resource state – Useful behavior.

Sensory acuity – How to use our senses to make distinctions between different bits of incoming information.

Sorting polarities – Something that makes a person drift in opposite directions at once.

Stacking anchors – Same anchors in different resources.

Strategy – The approach and pattern of behavioral steps, which lead to a specific outcome.

Submodalities – The subdivisions of the representational systems.

The NLP techniques and life experience made easy to understand in a simple way

----

A personal development self-study book for prosperity and success.

It is not luck that transforms people to higher levels; there are definite, known techniques to achieve success.

If you want guiding techniques help you get more energy, positive thoughts, joy, and passion to achieve success and overcome the negative impacts of life, you need *NLP FOR LIFE SUCCESS.*